D1576223

*A Gift for*

_____

*Presented by*

_____

# *I Used to*
# *Know That*
# SHAKESPEARE

All the world's a stage,
And all the men and women merely players.
They have their exits and their entrances,
And one man in his time plays many parts.

*As You Like It* 2.7.139–142

# I Used to Know That

# SHAKESPEARE

## stuff you forgot from school

LIZ EVERS

Reader's
Digest

The Reader's Digest Association, Inc.
New York, NY / Montreal

A READER'S DIGEST BOOK

Copyright © 2011 Michael O'Mara Books Limited

First published in Great Britain as *To Be or Not to Be…* in 2010 by Michael O'Mara Books Limited, 9 Lion Yard, Tremadoc Road, London SW4 7NQ

Interior Designer: Ana Bjezanceric
Cover Designer: George McKeon

READER'S DIGEST TRADE PUBLISHING
U.S. Project Editor: Rebecca Behan
Copy Editor: Barbara Booth
Project Production Coordinator: Nick Anderson
Senior Art Director: George McKeon
Executive Editor, Trade Publishing: Dolores York
Manufacturing Manager: Elizabeth Dinda
Associate Publisher, Trade Publishing: Rosanne McManus
President and Publisher, Trade Publishing: Harold Clarke

Library of Congress Cataloging-in-Publication Data:
Evers, Liz.
 I used to know that. Shakespeare : stuff you forgot from school / Liz Evers.
    p. cm.
 Includes bibliographical references and index.
 ISBN 978-1-60652-246-2
 1. Shakespeare, William, 1564-1616--Handbooks, manuals, etc. I. Title.
 PR2894.E84 2011
 822.3'3--dc22

2010046593

# Contents

# Contents

# Contents

# Introduction

What does some dead guy from sixteenth-century Britain have to say about life today? Well, if you've ever compared someone to a summer's day or fallen prey to jealousy's "green-eyed monster"—that's Shakespeare. If you've ever been young and angst-ridden, Shakespeare's *Hamlet* beat you to it. And if you've ever told a "Knock, knock" joke—you guessed it—that's Shakespeare, too.

As both poet and playwright, William Shakespeare forever changed the English language and theater—and so became responsible for what may have seemed like an inordinate number of school assignments. Some people may remember fondly how Shakespeare's sonnets complemented the first stirrings of love in their hearts. Others may harbor bitterness at being forced in school to memorize his lengthy speeches. Yet others may have only dim recollections of desperate teenage lovers, of some depressed guy with a skull talking about death all the time, or the piles of bodies that seem to end up on the stage when the curtains close. Regardless, most people will acknowledge that they've forgotten most of what they once knew about Shakespeare.

This book fills in all the hazy details—and you don't have to interpret Elizabethan English. (Who speaks in iambic pentameter, anyway?) Individual synopses for each play explain all the major players, plotlines, and gossip. There's even a glossary of major characters, so finally you can keep straight the long-lost twins Antipholus of Ephesus and Antipholus of Syracuse (giving you an edge over the often confounded characters in *The Comedy of Errors*).

An index of famous one-liners provides handy reference for sparkling cocktail conversations; chapters on common quotations and words Shakespeare "invented" capture the scale of the Bard's influence; and, with its section on poetry, this book will hopefully stir up some romance—and maybe a little intrigue, too.

In this book, you'll discover the ins and outs of all Shakespeare's scandals. From a shotgun wedding to questions of adultery, homosexuality, "stolen" poems, and real estate shenanigans, William Shakespeare still keeps us guessing. Some scholars wonder whether even his true identity has been kept secret. But after all, as Juliet once mused, "What's in a name?" Shakespeare's got more passionate love scenes, villainous treachery, comedic mishaps, and happy endings than a summer blockbuster. Just turn the pages and enjoy.

# "What a piece of
# work is a man"

# The Life of
# William Shakespeare

No other writer has had such an influence on the English theater . . . and indeed on theater across the Western canon. Yet, Shakespeare had no biographer in his lifetime and what we do know about him has been cobbled together from a scattering of documents or inferred from his writing. He was born to John Shakespeare, a glover and later a bailiff, and John's wife Mary, in Stratford-upon-Avon, England, on or around April 23, 1564. It is presumed that as a son of a prominent local citizen he would have attended the nearby King's Free Grammar School to receive lessons in Latin and Greek.

Shakespeare married Anne Hathaway in 1582, when he was eighteen years old. She was twenty-six and expecting the first of their three children. This age difference and the fact that Anne was already pregnant has led some to wonder if it was a shotgun wedding forced by the Hathaway family.

Documents from the Episcopal Register at Worcester record the issuing of a wedding license to a "Wm Shaxpere" and an "Annam Whateley." The following day's entry shows that Hathaway relatives from Stratford signed a surety of £40 (about US $60) to guarantee the wedding of a "William Shag-spere" to "Anne Hathwey." One biographer, Frank Harris, claims that rather than just poor spelling, this is to be taken as evidence that Shakespeare was involved with two women—and wanted to marry the former but was forced to take the latter. Either way, Miss Hathaway became Mrs. Shakespeare in November, 1582, and their first child, Susanna, was born six months later. The couple then had twins, Hamnet and Judith, in February 1585, though of the two only Judith survived to adulthood.

## *The playwright*

After the birth of the twins little is known about Shakespeare's life; however, it is safe to assume that he moved to London in the mid to late 1580s and became established enough in the theater by 1592 for fellow dramatist Robert Greene in his *Groat's Worth of Wit* to call him: "an upstart crow, beautified with our feathers . . . supposes he is as well able to bombast out a blank verse as the best of you; and, being an absolute Johannes factotum [Jack of all trades], is in his own conceit the only Shake-scene in a country."

Throughout the 1590s and the first decade of the seventeenth century, Shakespeare enjoyed great success as a playwright. Shakespeare acted too—though it is assumed he largely took minor roles.

His company started off as the Chamberlain's Men, performing mainly at The Theatre in Shoreditch, London's first public theatre. The company then moved into the newly built

Globe Theatre in Southwark in 1599, which was owned by the company members, including Shakespeare, as shareholders. His company performed first before Queen Elizabeth I and then her successor, James I (James VI of Scotland). Under the royal patronage of James I, Shakespeare's theater company became known as the King's Men and performed at court some eleven times. From 1608, the company also performed at the indoor Blackfriars Theatre in the winter months.

## Shakespeare's theatre

Most of us have at some time studied at least one of Shakespeare's plays. Titles such as *King Lear, Hamlet, Macbeth, The Merchant of Venice, Richard III, Romeo and Juliet, Othello,* and *A Midsummer Night's Dream* will bring (hopefully pleasant) classroom memories flooding back to many. But Shakespeare never intended his plays to be studied; they were to be performed—and performed under conditions so entirely different to our modern experience of theater that it is hard to connect the two, even in the authentic environment of the rebuilt Globe in London.

Much is written about the raucous Elizabethan and Jacobean theater-going rabble, the ubiquitous clowns, and the boy actors playing maids, wives, and mothers (which incidentally was a uniquely British habit: women had begun playing women in other European countries long before). Perhaps the difference between historical and modern performances of Shakespeare is best illustrated by the fact that the plays generally ended with a bawdy song and a jig led by the company's clown. It didn't matter what the play was—the twittering *Twelfth Night* or the bloody tragedy *Titus Andronicus*—all characters alive or "dead" danced merrily at the play's conclusion. Can you imagine that happening in a contemporary performance of *Hamlet*? It would be surreal to say the least.

# The family man

How frequently Shakespeare returned to see his wife and children in Stratford we do not know. The lengthy periods of separation have led many to conjecture that it was an unhappy marriage. Others believe he visited between theatrical seasons and that the fact that he effectively retired there from 1612 is evidence of a strong familial bond.

Shakespeare is thought to have had a number of affairs while living his separate life in London, and his sonnets are frequently taken as evidence of this. With regard to the happiness or unhappiness of his marriage, the most frequently cited documentation of Shakespeare's disregard for his wife is his will. In it, Shakespeare appears to leave her only the "second best bed." I say *appears* as it may be the case that she would have automatically inherited up to a third of his estate regardless. That aside, many have seen this bequest as a slight upon Anne. More optimistic scholars have seen the bed as a knowing gift from husband to wife, as in all likelihood, the second-best bed was their marriage bed, the best being reserved for guests.

Shakespeare's remaining estate was bequeathed to his two daughters, the bulk of it going to the elder, Susanna. Both his daughters married but between them produced only one grandchild, Susanna's daughter Elizabeth, who herself died childless, leaving Shakespeare with no direct descendents, or legitimate ones that we know of at least.

## *Shakespeare's legacy*

Only 230 plays survive from the presumably thousands that were written during Shakespeare's time, meaning that a whopping twenty percent of them are ascribed to the Bard.

It all started back in 1623, seven years after Shakespeare's death, when two former members of his theater company, John Heminges and Henry Condell, published the so-called First Folio—Shakespeare's first collected works. Printed as *Mr William Shakespeare's Comedies, Histories & Tragedies*, the folio contained thirty-six of his plays pieced together from the memories of the actors who first played them, existing quarto editions of individual works, and other sources, possibly including theatrical cue sheets. Other folios followed, adding and subtracting plays along the way, but the First Folio supplied the most reliable source for at least twenty of the plays in the existing canon.

The thirty-eight plays outlined in this book are widely considered to be either entirely by Shakespeare or collaborative works with other playwrights. There are lots of opinions, but a chronology of the plays based on a number of different sources looks something like this:

## Early period (1588–1595)

- *The Two Gentlemen of Verona*

- *The Taming of the Shrew*

- *The Comedy of Errors*

- *Henry VI, Parts 1, 2, and 3*
  (*Part I* possibly written with Thomas Nashe)

- *King John*

- *Titus Andronicus*
  (possibly written with George Peele)

- *Richard III*

## Middle period (1596–1602: Elizabethan)

- *The Merchant of Venice*

- *A Midsummer Night's Dream*

- *Love's Labour's Lost*

- *Richard II*

- *Henry IV, Parts 1 and 2*

## "What a piece of work is a man"

- *The Merry Wives of Windsor*

- *Romeo and Juliet*

- *Much Ado About Nothing*

- *Henry V*

- *As You Like It*

- *Julius Caesar*

- *Twelfth Night*

- *Hamlet*

## Middle period (1603–1606: Jacobean)

- *Troilus and Cressida*

- *Othello*

- *Measure for Measure*

- *King Lear*

- *All's Well That Ends Well*

- *Macbeth*

- *Antony and Cleopatra*

- *Coriolanus*

## Late period (1607–1613)

- *Pericles* (with George Wilkins)

- *Timon of Athens* (with Thomas Middleton)

- *The Winter's Tale*

- *The Tempest*

- *Cymbeline*

- *The Two Noble Kinsmen* (with John Fletcher)

- *Henry VIII* (with John Fletcher)

## Note:

You will find synopses of all thirty-eight plays in the accepted canon broken down by period throughout this book.

## *"To be or not to be?"*

Many have questioned whether William Shakespeare, son of a rural glover, could have written such imaginative, exotic plays—conjuring places he'd never been to and writing histories of the great and good (and bad). He wasn't well traveled or university educated. However, most of his plays were based on existing texts and histories—and are historically inaccurate, anyway.

But theories that Shakespeare couldn't have been Shakespeare started to pop up in the 1700s. There are no records of anyone questioning the plays' authorship during the Jacobean era. The best-known alternate candidates for "Shakespeare" are the scientist, philosopher, and statesman Francis Bacon and the playwright Christopher Marlowe. Others include the earls of Derby, Essex, Oxford, and Rutland, and there even have been suggestions that Queen Elizabeth herself might have penned the Shakespeare plays. In the cases of Marlowe and Edward De Vere, earl of Oxford, quite a leap of faith is required, as both died before many of the plays were produced.

Let's not take that leap and instead think of the country boy who left his young family to come to the big city with aspirations to become an actor and even a playwright—just as the theater was burgeoning into the most popular form of mass entertainment and just before it was put down again by sour-faced Puritans. Into this small but hugely significant window of time stepped William Shakespeare to make his indelible mark on theater, literature, and language the world over.

# Timeline of Shakespeare's life

1564—Baptized on April 26

1582—Marries Anne Hathaway

1583—First daughter, Susanna, is born

1585—Twins Judith and Hamnet are born

1586-1591—Known as "the lost years," there are no records mentioning Shakespeare from this time

1592—First mention of him as a playwright in *Groat's Worth of Wit*

1595—Officially recorded as a member of the Chamberlain's Men

1596—His son Hamnet dies

1598—Quarto editions of some of the plays start appearing

1599—His theater company begins performances in the newly built Globe Theatre

1603—Performs before Queen Elizabeth; Chamberlain's Men become King's Men

1609—*Shakes-peares Sonnets* is published, possibly without his consent

1612—Known to be living in Stratford-upon-Avon

1614—Last play, *The Two Noble Kinsmen*, is completed

1616—Shakespeare dies April 23

# "And thereby hangs a tale"

# Shakespeare's Plays 1588–1595

Although no one can be certain of the exact dates when Shakespeare wrote many of his plays, a considerable amount of scholarship has gone into trying to accurately determine an approximate time period for each one.

## *The Two Gentlemen of Verona*

Love, elopement, deceit, cross-dressing, lust, multiple broken promises, misunderstandings, disguises, and a comedy dog—Shakespeare's first play has the lot. When it comes to matters of the heart, it seems that young men's behavior becomes less than gentlemanly.

### First half

When restless young Valentine heads to Milan to seek his fortune, his best friend Proteus stays in Verona to be near his beloved Julia. However, following a misunderstanding with his father, Proteus is sent to Milan on the heels of his friend. Before he leaves, he and Julia swear fidelity to each other and exchange rings.

Heartbroken by her loss, Julia resolves to follow Proteus to Milan. In true Shakespearian style she decides the best way to do this is disguised as a boy.

In Milan we catch up with Valentine, who has fallen head over heels for Silvia, daughter of the duke of Milan. When Proteus arrives on the scene he and Valentine compare their loves and try to outdo each other in their ardor. Proteus agrees to help Valentine and Silvia elope. However, once Proteus sets eyes on Silvia, he has a rather sudden change of heart. The best friend turns backstabber and decides to tell Silvia's father, the duke, of the young couple's elopement plans. The duke responds by banishing the love-struck Valentine from his court.

## Second half

With Valentine banished to the forest of outlaws, Proteus sets out to woo Silvia. He sends Sebastian, a boy in his employ, to deliver a ring to his new beloved. Sebastian is, of course, Julia in disguise, and the ring is the very one she gave Proteus in Verona.

Silvia runs away to escape her unwanted and rather aggressive suitor, Proteus, and is captured by outlaws. As luck would have it, Valentine has shot up the ranks to become leader of the outlaws after just a few days in the forest, but he chooses to remain incognito for a little while longer. Proteus arrives, pleading with and then threatening Silvia, and is finally challenged by his former friend Valentine. Proteus begs forgiveness from Valentine—and gets it—something that causes Sebastian to faint and thus reveal himself as Julia. Proteus instantly (and rather conveniently) forgets the whole Silvia thing and is delighted to see his first love again. She forgives him, too. The duke gives his blessing to the union of Valentine and Silvia and both couples wed.

# The Taming of the Shrew

This story of a spirited single woman being transformed into a meek, submissive wife may rankle with many a contemporary playgoer. However, for all its casual sexism, *The Taming of the Shrew* is still one of Shakespeare's best-loved comedies.

## First half

The action unfolds in Padua where three suitors of varying quality vie for the hand of beautiful Bianca, daughter of the wealthy Baptista. Of the three, Lucentio is the most ardent (as well as the youngest and prettiest). Baptista, however, has another daughter, the elder Katherine, whom he insists must be married before Bianca. The only problem is that Katherine doesn't want to marry anyone—and what's more, nobody wants to marry her. When she's not slapping her sister, she's screaming or smashing lutes over the servants' heads.

Then the mercenary, cash-strapped, and devilishly charming Petruchio arrives on the scene and, spurred on by Bianca's other suitors Gremio and Hortensio, sets about wooing the wild-natured Katherine. With a smooth tongue Petruchio quickly negotiates dowry terms with Baptista and sets out to confuse Kate (his new name for her) into submission. He arrives late to his own wedding and dressed in rags, saying marriage is a solemn affair and not about finery, but then goes on to strike the priest and throw cake and wine at the sexton. His next move is to refuse to attend the wedding banquet and instead whisks Kate off to his home in Verona, where he doesn't feed her for a couple of days on the pretext that the food offered isn't good enough for her. He curses and strikes his servants for good measure, too.

## Second half

All the while Kate is being worn down or "tamed" (or brainwashed) by her new husband's unpredictable and cruel behavior. On the road back to Padua, Petruchio tests out his handiwork and finds that his wife will agree with him that day is night and that an elderly gent is in fact, a young woman.

In Padua, after various twists and turns involving duplicity, disguises, and some identity swapping, Bianca and Lucentio are wed. Thereafter he, Petruchio, and the also recently married Hortensio, discuss the subject of obedience in a wife. While both Bianca and Hortensio's wife fail to come to their husbands when called, Kate shows them up by responding instantly to Petruchio's call. She dutifully comes running to her master and at his command speaks passionately about how women are "bound to serve, love and obey." . . . No irony, no twist—that's how the play ends. Well, actually that's not quite how it ends. It ends with Petruchio uttering the famous line "Come on, and kiss me, Kate," before taking his subservient new bride off to bed. Fingers crossed they lived happily ever after. I have my doubts.

*The Taming of the Shrew* is thought to have also gone by the name *Love's Labour's Won*, a sort of companion to *Love's Labour's Lost* (see page 66).

Although you might think that modern audiences would be put off by the idea of a husband breaking his wife's spirit, adaptations of *The Taming of the Shrew* have proved successful throughout the twentieth century. Cole Porter's musical comedy *Kiss Me Kate* wowed audiences first in 1948 and then in a revival in 2000, productions that won five Tony Awards each.

Breakout performances by Julia Stiles and Heath Ledger in the 1999 film *10 Things I Hate About You* made Shakespeare's convoluted plot accessible to teenagers, with the drama set in the fictional, modern-day Padua High School.

# The Comedy of Errors

This play is considered by many to be Shakespeare's first comedy (thought to be written in 1593) and, at 1,786 lines, it is also his shortest play. He manages to pack quite a lot of action in though—remembering who's who and what's what in this comedy of mistaken identity and endless misunderstanding is no mean feat. I'll try to keep it as simple as I can. . . .

## First half

The merchant Egeon and his wife are far away from their home of Syracuse when she gives birth to identical twin sons.

At the same time, in the same inn, another considerably poorer woman is giving birth to twin boys, too. Taking pity on the impoverished new mother, Egeon buys her babies with the intention of raising them as servants to his own sons.

But, as they sail for home, their ship is caught in a ferocious storm and the family is separated—the mother with one son and servant-to-be, and Egeon with the other two.

When they turn eighteen, Egeon's duo set off on a quest to find the missing mother and their respective brothers. After many years, their search brings them to Ephesus—where Egeon is in turn searching for them, and where their brothers are indeed resident, one a prosperous citizen, and the other, well, still his servant.

By confusing coincidence, both of Egeon's sons are called Antipholus, while their respective servants share the name Dromio.

Still with me?

## Second half

So Antipholus and his Dromio of Syracuse have arrived in Ephesus, weary of their fruitless search for their respective brothers and Antipholus's mother. Within a very short space of time they are both mistaken for their twin counterparts. They take in stride the strange behavior of people towards them, as Ephesus is known as a place of enchantment and sorcery.

Antipholus of Syracuse is treated regally in the streets by strangers—he's even given jewels. Dromio however, feels the wrath of his "master" Antipholus of Ephesus for not carrying out his orders. Dromio of Ephesus gets a thrashing from

Antipholus of Syracuse for similar disobedience. Adriana, wife of Antipholus of Ephesus, mistakes Antipholus of Syracuse for her husband—but he falls in love with her sister Luciana. Antipholus of Ephesus is arrested for debt after a skirmish with a goldsmith who gave his twin a gold chain he had ordered—and he's branded a lunatic to boot. It's all terribly confusing and hilarious by turns, with lashings of slapstick violence thrown in (for the Dromios at least).

Pursued and generally baffled, Antipholus of Syracuse heads to the same abbey where his father Egeon is also taking refuge, and the two are reunited. It also happily turns out that the abbess is Egeon's long-lost wife. All family members are finally joyously reunited, and Antipholus of Syracuse marries his brother's sister-in-law, Luciana.

## Henry VI, Parts 1, 2, and 3

Shakespeare's trilogy of history plays, *Henry VI*, parts 1, 2, and 3 depict the reign of King Henry VI, between 1422 and 1445. The plays touch on the young Henry's ascension to the throne, his marriage to the French princess Margaret of Anjou, and the ongoing power struggle for the English throne.

### Part 1

Child-king Henry has just inherited the throne but is too young to govern so Humphrey, Duke of Gloucester, acts as Protector, while Henry Beaufort occupies the high office of

Bishop of Winchester. These two men jostle for position while the English army fights Joan of Arc to retain the power won by the king's late father, Henry V, in France.

After Joan's execution, Henry cements peace with France by marrying the French princess Margaret of Anjou. Taking plenty of historical license, Shakespeare casts Margaret as an adulteress who is having an affair with the king's ambassador to France, the Earl of Suffolk.

This play introduces the Wars of the Roses between the noble houses of York and Lancaster that would dominate, and ultimately end, Henry's reign.

## Part 2

The Wars of the Roses are in full swing, and we find that Henry has grown into a weak and easily manipulated adult, whose wife, Margaret, rules at home with the aid of her lover, the Earl of Suffolk. Margaret and Suffolk conspire against Gloucester, whose power is a threat to their ambitions, claiming that his wife consorts with witches. At the battle of St Albans, Richard of York's son (the future Richard III) kills his family's main adversary, Somerset, and thus ends the thirty-year-long Wars of the Roses. Following this success York plans to go after the king, who is pretty much at his mercy.

Suffolk is executed for the murder of Gloucester, and the queen mourns her dead lover in a memorably macabre scene in which she cradles his decapitated head in her lap.

## Part 3

Henry agrees to allow the House of York to succeed him on the throne, thus disinheriting his son Edward, Prince of Wales. However, taking matters into her own hands, Queen Margaret leads the royal army to victory over York and has him executed. The fallen Duke's sons, including the future Richard III, raise a new army and retake power. During that battle, Edward is killed on the battlefield, while King Henry is murdered in the Tower of London.

The House of York accedes to the throne with its own Edward as king. But all is not well within that family as Edward's brother Richard has his own ideas about who should wear the crown. This final part of the trilogy segues nicely into *Richard III* (see page 36).

Throughout the three plays, Henry VI is portrayed as a weak yet moral man who stands out virtuously next to his power-crazed adversaries. His goodness makes him a tragic figure and someone who has had greatness thrust upon him. Having been declared king at just six months old, poor Henry never stood a chance.

## *King John*

Not a common play on curricula or in performance, this neglected early history play tells the tale of a flawed, incompetent, and rather dangerous king. Historically, John was the brother of the much-revered Richard the Lionheart, and essentially stole the throne from its rightful heir, Richard's young son Arthur—whom in all likelihood he then had murdered.

John reigned for seventeen years in the early thirteenth century, during which time he was forced to sign the Magna Carta, limiting the absolute power of the monarchy. This last fact is not mentioned in the play.

In Shakespeare's drama, John is universally disliked and distrusted. Philip, king of France, wants the saintly young Arthur on the throne and the situation escalates into war, resolved with marriage pacts and by giving Arthur a dukedom. Next John falls foul of the Pope in Rome when he refuses to accept the Pope's candidate for the role of Archbishop of Canterbury. John is excommunicated from the Church and then, encouraged by the scorned Pope, the French invade England. Arthur is imprisoned and dies trying to escape (rather than being murdered as is historically believed). John is defeated in battle, although the French ultimately retreat. He learns of this on his deathbed and his son is crowned Henry III.

## *Titus Andronicus*

Rape, mutilation, cannibalism—this play is awash with blood and gore from the outset and was a big hit for Shakespeare as a consequence. Taking the hugely popular sixteenth-century format of the revenge tragedy, the play's trajectory is defined by the required death of most of its characters, minor and major, in a bloody finale.

## First half

Despite some historic-seeming references, this play and its characters are entirely fictitious. It takes ancient Rome as its setting, where Titus, a Roman war hero, returns from a long campaign against the Goths. He brings with him valuable prisoners of war—the Goth queen Tamora, her three sons, and her lover, Aaron the Moor. To placate the ghosts of his many sons killed in battle, and in accordance with Roman tradition, Titus sacrifices Tamora's eldest.

The people of Rome want Titus for their new emperor but instead he recommends Saturninus, who asks to marry Titus's daughter Lavinia. She, however, is in love with Saturninus's brother Bassianus, and he promptly "kidnaps" her to save her from the proposed marriage. Saturninus then falls for the Goth queen Tamora and the two are married, putting her in a dangerous new position of power.

Tamora's two remaining sons, with the assistance of Aaron the Moor, murder Bassianus and trap and implicate two of Titus's sons, Quintus and Martius. Tamora's sons then rape Lavinia and, to silence her, cut off her tongue and hands. Emperor Saturninus does not believe that Titus's sons are innocent of his brother's murder but tells the old warrior, via Aaron the Moor, that if he sends his hand to him, he will pardon and release Quintus and Martius. Titus duly makes this sacrifice and sends his hand to Saturninus but in return is sent back the severed heads of his sons. On top of coping with the rape and mutilation of his daughter, this cruel trick brings Titus close to madness.

## Second half

Unable to communicate by any other means, Lavinia writes the names of her attackers in sand for her father to read. While Titus plots his revenge, his eldest son Lucius heads off to gather an army against the emperor and his wicked wife.

Not content with a commonplace killing, Titus slits the throats of the queen's sons and bakes parts of their bodies in pies. He then serves them up to their mother and her husband at a banquet. There he stabs his daughter Lavinia, to end her shame at being raped, and murders Tamora. In response Saturninus kills Titus and is in turn killed by Lucius. Now the only member of a noble family left alive, Lucius is elected emperor. But that doesn't put an end to the killing spree. Lucius then orders that Aaron the Moor be buried to the neck and starved to death and that the body of Tamora be thrown to wild animals.

Quentin Tarantino still has a lot to learn from the old Bard.

Some scholars believe that the play was written by or with George Peele—mainly because of this particular playwright's penchant for gore. He's sometimes named as the author or co-author of *Henry VI, Parts 1* and *2*, too.

# Richard III

One of Shakespeare's most notorious villains, the hunchbacked Richard III is not plagued by minor things like conscience. Instead, he embraces his wickedness and, by addressing the audience directly, makes us complicit in it.

This is the history play in which Shakespeare takes the most license. It was designed to vindicate Henry VII, the grandfather of the then-reigning Queen Elizabeth I, who took his throne through force of arms. For Henry to be seen as an honorable man and the progenitor of an honorable dynasty, Richard III had to be demonized. There is doubt whether Richard was responsible for most of the deaths Shakespeare attributes to him and if he even had any physical deformity.

## First half

Picking up where *Henry VI, Part 3,* left off, this blood-soaked play finds the power-hungry Richard, Duke of Gloucester, embarking on a path of manipulation and murder to steal the throne. He deceives his brother, the reigning but very ill King Edward IV, into arresting their brother Clarence. He then deceives Clarence by insisting that he is on his side and that he will intercede on his behalf—and then has him murdered.

In the preceding play *(Henry VI)* Richard was responsible for the deaths of both the king and his heir, Edward. Now Richard has set his cap at Lady Anne, Edward's widow, wooing her literally over her father-in-law's corpse. He convinces her of his repentance for past crimes, and she becomes his wife— though in an aside Richard assures us it won't be for long.

Edward IV's ill health and distress at the death of Clarence gets the better of him and he dies, leaving his two sons, the Prince of Wales and Duke of York, standing between Richard and the throne. He has the boys installed in the royal quarters at the Tower of London and instructs Buckingham to spread the word that they are illegitimate and that King Edward was illegitimate, too. Once those seeds are sown, Buckingham gathers a delegation of citizens to "beg" Richard to take the throne as its legitimate heir. With great theatricality Richard refuses, only to humbly assent to their wishes shortly thereafter.

## Second half

Not content with stealing their birthright, the new King Richard orders the deaths of his nephews in the Tower and then spreads word that his wife, Anne, is dying (and soon after has her dispatched, too). Richard has now set his sights on his brother Edward's daughter, Elizabeth, for his next wife.

In the meantime, the Earl of Richmond is the great hope to vanquish Richard. He leads an army to face the king at Bosworth Field. The night before the battle, both Richmond and Richard are visited by the ghosts of all of those Richard has killed, blessing and cursing the men respectively. During the battle, Richard loses his horse but fights bravely on, until he is confronted and killed by Richmond ("A horse! A horse! My kingdom for a horse."). Richmond is crowned Henry VII and announces that he will marry Elizabeth, thus bringing the long Wars of the Roses to an end and ushering in the new reign of the Tudors.

# "Words, words, words"

# Shakespeare's
# Language Legacy

It's hard to grasp the impact that this single writer had on the English language as we know it. Shakespeare played with words, turning verbs into nouns, tacking on prefixes and suffixes, and mixing and matching words and phrases together to create new ideas and build upon the language's existing framework.

## *Everyday words*
## *we owe to Shakespeare*

When we think of Shakespeare, we often think of his wit and wordplay. His characters revel in puns, double entendres, and more insults than one might have thought possible. (The Earl of Kent unfurls his disdain for the schemes against King Lear, for example, using more than twenty consecutive insults, including such creative gems as "lily-livered," "worsted-stocking," and "whoreson.")

By the calculations of the *Oxford English Dictionary* and David and Ben Crystal's *The Shakespeare Miscellany*, there are 357 instances where Shakespeare is the only recorded user of a word in one or more of its senses. There are a further 1,035 instances where Shakespeare likely introduced or popularized the words. There are also another 642 instances where Shakespeare is the first of several people to use a word, but other uses occur within twenty-five years, and therefore it is less likely that he was the first to introduce the word.

If all of these words are accepted as Shakespeare's then that's 2,034 (or 1,392 if we exclude the last category), about 800 of which have survived to the present day. Whatever way you look at it, that's an awful lot of words. Shakespeare brought new meaning to existing stems by introducing the prefixes *dis-*, *un-*, *im-*, and *in-* or adding the suffix *-less*. Examples of these are included in the selection below.

- abstemious (*The Tempest*, from the Latin meaning "to abstain from alcohol." Its meaning extended to include sexual behaviors, too)

- accommodation (*Othello*)

- accused (*Richard II*; it is the first known use of the word as a noun, meaning "the person accused of a crime")

- addiction (*Henry V* and *Othello*)

- aerial (*Othello*)

## "Words, words, words"

- alligator (*Romeo and Juliet*; the Spanish *aligarto* was already in use)

- to arouse (*Henry VI, Part 2* and *Hamlet*; *to rouse* was the usual form)

- assassination (*Macbeth*; *assassin* was already in use)

- auspicious (this appears in many plays and comes from *auspice*, the Roman practice of fortune-telling by bird flight; *inauspicious* appears in *Romeo and Juliet*)

- bandit (*Henry VI, Part 2*, from the Italian *bandetto*)

- baseless (*The Tempest*, meaning "groundless, fantasy")

- bedazzled (*The Taming of the Shrew*)

- bedroom (*A Midsummer Night's Dream*)

- belongings (*Measure for Measure*)

- to besmirch (*Henry V*)

- birthplace (*Coriolanus*)

- bloodstained (*Henry IV, Part 1*)

- to cake (*Timon of Athens*, first known use as a verb)

- to cater (*As You Like It,* meaning "a buyer of provisions")

- to champion (*Macbeth,* first known use as a verb)

- cold-blooded (*King John,* meaning "lacking emotion")

- cold-hearted (*Antony and Cleopatra*)

- deafening (*Henry IV, Part 2*)

- disgraceful (*Henry VI, Part 1,* meaning "not graceful")

- dishearten (*Henry V*)

- to dislocate (*King Lear,* referring to anatomy)

- distasteful (*Timon of Athens*)

- domineering (*Love's Labour's Lost*)

- downstairs (*Henry IV, Part 1;* first use as an adjective)

- to drug (*Macbeth;* first known use as a verb)

- to educate (*Love's Labour's Lost*)

- to elbow (*King Lear;* first use as a verb)

- to ensnare (*Othello*)

- eventful (*As You Like It*)

- eyeball (*The Tempest*)

- farmhouse (*The Merry Wives of Windsor*, first known use of the compound)

- fashionable (*Timon of Athens* and *Troilus and Cressida*)

- fitful (*Macbeth*)

- flawed (*King Lear*, first use as an adjective)

- flowery (*A Midsummer Night's Dream*)

- foppish (*King Lear*)

- fortune-teller (*The Comedy of Errors*)

- gnarled (*Measure for Measure*, from *knurled* meaning "bumpy")

- to gossip (*The Comedy of Errors*; first use as a verb)

- hint (*Othello*; first use in today's sense)

- to humor (*Love's Labour's Lost*; first use as a verb)

- impartial (*Henry IV, Part 2*)

- inaudible (*All's Well That Ends Well*; *audible* was already in use)

- lackluster (*As You Like It*)

- laughable (*The Merchant of Venice*)

- leaky (*Antony and Cleopatra* and *The Tempest*)

- marketable (*As You Like It*; first use as adjective)

- mimic (*A Midsummer Night's Dream*)

- moonbeam (*A Midsummer Night's Dream*)

- mortifying (*Merchant of Venice* and *Much Ado About Nothing*)

- motionless (*Henry V*)

- multitudinous (*Macbeth*)

- new-fangled (*Love's Labour's Lost* and *As You Like It*)

- pageantry (*Pericles*)

## "Words, words, words"

- perplex (*King John* and *Cymbeline*)

- to petition (*Antony and Cleopatra* and *Coriolanus*; first uses as a verb)

- published (*Henry VI, Part 2*)

- reclusive (*Much Ado About Nothing*)

- sanctimonious (*Measure for Measure* and *The Tempest*)

- satisfying (*Othello* and *Cymbeline*)

- savagery (*King John* and *Henry V*)

- schoolboy (*Julius Caesar* and *Much Ado About Nothing*)

- silliness (*Othello*)

- to submerge (*Antony and Cleopatra*)

- unchanging (*The Merchant of Venice*)

- uncomfortable (*Romeo and Juliet*)

- unearthly (*The Winter's Tale*)

- unmitigated (*Much Ado About Nothing*)

- well behaved (*The Merry Wives of Windsor*)
- well bred (*Henry IV, Part 2*)
- well read (*Henry IV, Part 1*)
- widowed (*Sonnet 97* and *Coriolanus*)

Of course, you won't find every word that Shakespeare dreamed up in the dictionary, and a large number never quite caught on. Some of my favorites include *begnaw* (to bite or eat away), *dispunge* (to erase—or to squeeze out like a spunge, I'm not kidding!), and *fracted* (broken).

And here are some other words that Shakespeare may have coined but which have not passed into common use: *attasked*, *bubukles*, *congreeing*, *conspectuities*, *immoment*, *incorpsed*, *jointing*, *mistempered*, *oppugnancy*, *palmy*, *plantage*, *propugnation*, *relume*, *reprobance*, *rubious*, *smilets*, *supplyment*, and *unsisting*.

You can find meanings for these words in some dictionaries, but I think it's just as fun to come up with your own. Perhaps *bubukles* perfectly describes somewhat chubby ankles or your grandma's perfectly delicious breakfast pastries. Go ahead and play around—Shakespeare would definitely approve.

# Everyday phrases we owe to Shakespeare

A huge number of common phrases in use today are derived from Shakespeare. *Hamlet* leads the way as the most inadvertently quoted play, featuring turns of phrase such as "in my heart of hearts," "in my mind's eye," and "it smells to heaven." *Macbeth* has spawned quite a few too, including "come what may," "the be-all and end-all," and "what's done is done." *Othello* has given us "a foregone conclusion," "wear my heart on my sleeve," and "neither here nor there." From plays about various kings called Henry we get "the game is afoot," (*Henry IV, Part 1*), "eaten me out of house and home" (*Henry IV, Part 2*), and "dead as a doornail" (*Henry VI, Part 2*). And just when you thought another great English writer might provide some competition, you discover that "what the dickens" is from Shakespeare's *The Merry Wives of Windsor*.

In the pages that follow you'll find a choice selection of other commonly used phrases and quotations that we owe to the rather prolific Mr. Shakespeare. . . .

## A Midsummer Night's Dream
    The course of true love never did run smooth

## As You Like It
    All the world's a stage

- Bag and baggage

- The working day world

- Too much of a good thing

- We have seen better days


## Hamlet

- Ay, there's the rub

- Brevity is the soul of wit (*wit* meant intelligence in its original context)

- Conscience does make cowards of us all

- [Every] Dog will have its day

- Frailty, thy name is woman

- Get thee to a nunnery

- In my heart of hearts

- In my mind's eye

- It smells to heaven

- More in sorrow than in anger

- Murder most foul

- Neither a borrower nor a lender be

- Not a mouse stirring

- Sweets to the sweet

- The apparel oft proclaim the man (now "the clothes make the man")

- The lady doth protest too much, methinks

- Though this be madness, yet there is method in't (now "method in his/her madness")

- To thine own self be true

- What a piece of work is a man

## Henry IV, Part 1

- Give the devil his due

❦ The better part of valor is discretion

❦ The game is afoot

## Henry IV, Part 2

❦ Eaten me out of house and home

❦ Uneasy lies the head that wears a crown

## Henry VI, Part 3

❦ Breathe one's last

❦ Dead as a doornail

❦ Smooth runs the water where the brook is deep

## Julius Caesar

❦ Beware the Ides of March

❦ Dish fit for the gods

❦ Et tu, Brute!

  It was Greek to me

  Let slip the dogs of war

  Stood on ceremonies

  Unkindest cut of all

## King John
  Cold comfort

  Elbow room

## King Lear
  Come full circle

  Every inch a king

  More sinned against than sinning

## Love's Labour's Lost
  Play fast and loose

  The naked truth

## Macbeth

- Come what may

- Crack of doom

- Full of sound and fury

- Milk of human kindness

- One fell swoop

- Sorry sight

- The be-all and the end-all

- What's done is done

### Knock, knock! Who's there? (*Macbeth*)

The knock-knock joke has traveled far and wide since Macduff and Lennox first pounded on the gate in *Macbeth*. In France the joke is known as *toc-toc*, while in Afrikaans and Dutch it is *klop-klop*. No doubt these variations are just as "hilarious."

## Othello

- A foregone conclusion

- Pomp and circumstance

- 'Tis neither here nor there

- Wear my heart on my sleeve

## Richard III

- A tower of strength

- Short shrift

- Spotless reputation

## Romeo and Juliet

- A fool's paradise

- Parting is such sweet sorrow

- Star-crossed lovers

- What's in a name?

**Green-eyed monster (*Othello*)**

The term *green-eyed* in reference to jealousy was first uttered by Portia in *The Merchant of Venice*, while the full expression *green-eyed monster* is spoken by the wicked Iago in the later *Othello*. Iago uses the phrase to "warn" Othello about the effects of jealousy—all the while deliberately stoking the emotion within him. In *Othello*, Shakespeare also refers to cats as green-eyed monsters in the way that they play with mice before killing them.

The color green was associated with sickness and unripe food that would upset the stomach. In *Antony and Cleopatra*, Shakespeare describes envy as the "green sickness," hence the phrase *green with envy*.

## The Comedy of Errors
❧ Something in the wind

## The Merry Wives of Windsor
❧ Laughing-stock

❧ Short and the long of it (now usually "the long and short of it")

- The world's mine oyster

- Throw cold water on it

- What the dickens

## The Merchant of Venice

- Bated breath

- Hold a candle to

- It's a wise father that knows his own child

- Love is blind

- My own flesh and blood

- The devil can cite Scripture for his purpose

- The quality of mercy is not strained

## The Taming of the Shrew

- An eye-sore

- Budge an inch

- Kill with kindness

- More fool you

## The Tempest
- Into thin air

- O brave new world

- Strange bedfellows

- We are such stuff as dreams are made on

## The Two Gentlemen of Verona
- To make a virtue of necessity

## The Winter's Tale
- As white as driven snow

## Troilus and Cressida
- Good riddance

# "The play's the thing"

# Shakespeare's Plays 1596–1602

This period, often referred to as Shakespeare's Second Period," was a prolific time for Shakespeare. Not only did he work as an actor and playwright but he also became a businessman, investing in the Globe Theatre, which was built in 1599. During this period, he created four of his most famous plays—Henry the Fifth, Julius Caesar, As You Like It, and Hamlet.

## *The Merchant of Venice*

Usually categorized as a comedy, this play's casual anti-Semitism is quite shocking to a modern audience. In the context of the time in which it was produced, however, the real surprise is that Shakespeare imbued the Jewish moneylender Shylock with any sympathetic characteristics at all, let alone gave him some of the play's most powerfully emotive speeches.

## First half

The merchant of the title is Antonio, who kick-starts the action by agreeing to finance his good friend Bassanio's marriage suit of the wealthy Portia of Belmont. Expecting his ships to return laden with goods, Antonio goes to the moneylender Shylock. Shylock, however, feels he has been greatly insulted by Antonio in the past and so, while agreeing to the loan, sets terms that he hopes will lead to Antonio's demise: if he cannot repay the loan at the allotted time, Antonio must give Shylock one pound of his own flesh.

Shylock's satisfaction at having struck such a bargain is cut short when his daughter Jessica runs away to be with her beloved Lorenzo, stealing Shylock's money and renouncing her religion to boot. Jessica and Lorenzo go to Belmont, the very place where Bassanio is about to attempt the challenge for Portia's hand. In accordance with Portia's father's wishes, every suitor (of which there are many) must choose one of three caskets in gold, silver, and lead. Upon opening the casket they learn whether they have won Portia.

Unlike the other suitors, Bassanio is not drawn by the false flash of gold and silver but instead opts for the more honest lead. Upon opening it, he finds a portrait of Portia—his beloved wife-to-be. As they celebrate their betrothal, news comes that Antonio's ships are lost and that he must by law comply with Shylock's forfeit.

## Second half

The couple quickly marry before Bassanio rushes to the side of Antonio. Seeing his distress, his new wife decides secretly to disguise herself as a lawyer, "Balthasar," and fight Antonio's case personally. She arrives just as Shylock is turning down the Duke of Venice's invitation to show mercy to Antonio. Balthasar, too, pleads for mercy, but again, Shylock refuses. Balthasar points out that the moneylender is entitled only to a pound of flesh—but not a single drop of "Christian blood." Realizing he cannot win, Shylock says he'll settle for three times the original money, but Balthasar then turns the tables on him. For attempting to take the life of a citizen he will lose all of his property. In a final insult, Antonio says that the property should go to Jessica and Lorenzo and that Shylock must become a Christian too.

In gratitude to Balthasar, Bassanio hands over the ring given to him by Portia, which she had told him must never leave his finger. Everyone returns to Belmont to celebrate. Portia immediately asks Bassanio for his ring, and when he has been made to feel sufficiently guilty, she reveals that she was Balthasar all along. Not only that but she produces a letter for Antonio, which reveals that three of his ships have survived and will be with him soon, loaded with goods. The play ends happily for everyone except poor old Shylock.

Debate continues about whether Shakespeare's portrayal of the villain Shylock is meant to endorse popular anti-Semitism of the time or expose it. Indeed, Shakespeare's characterization, though reliant upon stereotyping, is more nuanced than similar characters of his contemporaries.

It's worth noting that in London in 1594, a Portuguese Jew by the name of Dr. Roderigo Lopez was executed on a charge of attempting to poison a patient—one Queen Elizabeth I. Doubtless this play's punishment of the "evil" Jew would have appealed to the renewed anti-Semitism of Shakespeare's audience.

## A Midsummer Night's Dream

Though it's set in ancient Athens, the midsummer revels woven through with magic and enchantment in this play are uniquely English. This is one of Shakespeare's most-performed works and is jam-packed with colorful characters and memorable lines and scenes. Two separate stories unfold simultaneously in the forest—one human, one fairy.

## First half

Duke Theseus and his wife-to-be, Hippolyta, discuss their impending nuptials, but are constantly interrupted by problems from fellow Athenians. Egeus wants his daughter Hermia to marry Demetrius, but she's in love with Lysander. If Hermia disobeys her father she could face banishment or even death, so she takes a chance and runs off into the forest with Lysander. Meanwhile Hermia's friend Helena is in love with Demetrius, but he's only interested in the unobtainable Hermia. Demetrius pursues Hermia, and Helena pursues Demetrius.

In the meantime, a group of laborers, lead by Nick Bottom, discuss their rehearsals for their play *Pyramus and Thisbe* to be performed at Theseus's wedding. It is decided that they shall rehearse in the forest to avoid being watched by nosy Athenians.

Elsewhere, Oberon, king of the fairies, and his wife Titania quarrel over whose entourage a changeling boy will join. Oberon sends his servant Puck to find a magic flower to make a love charm for his wife so that she will fall in love with the first creature she sees.

While Puck is gone, Oberon overhears Demetrius tell Helena that he is sick at the sight of her. She responds that she would rather die than not keep following him. Oberon decides that the love charm might be put to use on this couple as well and dispatches Puck in pursuit of them.

Oberon casts his spell on Titania as she sleeps in the forest. Puck finds Lysander and Hermia and, mistaking them for the couple described by Oberon, sprinkles the charm onto

Lysander's eyelids. Soon afterwards Helena, pursuing Demetrius, awakens Lysander as she stops to rest. He instantly falls madly in love with her, and Hermia awakens a short while later to find herself alone. She begins an anxious search for her missing lover.

The mischievous Puck comes across the rehearsing actors and when Bottom is separated briefly from the group, Puck transforms his head into that of an ass. The oblivious Bottom returns to the group and scares them out of their wits, and then awakens the nearby Titania who falls instantly in love with him, ass head and all, and commands her servants to attend to his every wish.

## Second half

High jinks ensue as Oberon enchants Demetrius to fall in love with Helena as planned, and the once-scorned young woman has to deal with the attentions of two ardent suitors and a jealous Hermia. The men run off to duel, and Puck follows them to reverse the spell over Lysander.

Having won the changeling boy from Titania, Oberon lifts the spell from her eyes, and his befuddled wife awakens from her stupor talking about the visions she has had. Meanwhile, Theseus, out on his May Day hunt, enters the forest and finds the Athenians asleep. They're all rather confused but seem to be paired up happily, Lysander with Hermia and Demetrius with Helena. Theseus announces that they shall all be married. The ass head gone, a bewildered Bottom stumbles back to join his acting comrades to perform at Theseus's wedding.

Afterward, Theseus announces that it is the "fairy time" and so all go to bed. Oberon and Titania appear and bless the house of Theseus. Puck is last on stage to sign off with his speech intimating that everything the audience has witnessed has been but a dream.

*"If we shadows have offended,*
*Think but this, and all is mended,*
*That you have but slumbered here*
*While these visions did appear"* (5.1.417)

# Love's Labour's Lost

The play is set in Navarre, a place dedicated to learning and study. It is ruled over by King Ferdinand, who has vowed, along with his courtiers Berowne, Dumain, and Longaville, to devote himself to three years of study and self-denial, barring women from his court.

### First half

When the Princess of France and her entourage of beauties—Rosaline, Katherine, and Maria—show up on a diplomatic mission, the king's favorite courtiers forget their studies and instantly fall head over heels.

The bookish young men, however, delude themselves into believing that they are "studying" courtship and, toward that end, disguise themselves as visiting Russians to test their new ladies. In turn, the wily ladies confuse the courtiers by wearing masks and swapping jewelry, to be wooed by each other's love interests. Chaos and myriad misunderstandings ensue.

## Second half

The visiting Spanish dignitary Don Armado provides additional comic relief in the company of Costard the clown. Armado is a figure of ridicule and thought to be a playful human caricature of the defeated Spanish Armada of 1588. Armado and Costard both vie for the love of a woman named Jaquenetta.

Just as the play reaches its giddiest heights, news comes that the king of France has died, and so his daughter and her attendants have to leave. They tell their distraught lovers to live another year in their old secluded way until they come courting again. Recalling the seasons, the play ends with songs of spring and winter.

# Richard II

This play kick-starts the Henriad, the four-part play cycle that also includes *Henry IV, Parts I* and *II* and *Henry V*. It tells the tale of the downfall of a narcissistic yet fatalistic king and brings into question the legitimacy of divine right—that is, that those of royal blood are favored by God and should automatically inherit the throne.

## First half

The action of the play starts with the mishandling of the murder of the Duke of Gloucester, Richard's uncle. Richard's cousin Henry Bolingbroke insists that the Duke of Norfolk is responsible, and so Richard decrees that the matter be resolved with a joust. But the king then calls off the joust and banishes the two participants instead. When Bolingbroke's father dies, Richard seizes his cousin's inheritance to pay for a war in Ireland.

This does not go down well. With the support of Richard's disaffected lords, Bolingbroke returns and wages war against the king, who, after his defeat in Ireland, is forced to take refuge in Flint Castle in Wales. He is captured there, exiled to Yorkshire, and made to abdicate. With the king stripped of his power and Bolingbroke refusing to be named king, the Duke of York acts as regent. It's not long before supporters of Richard plot a rebellion but are discovered by Bolingbroke.

## Second half

In a memorably deadly (and historically inaccurate) scene, a dejected Bolingbroke asks, "Have I no friend will rid me of this living fear?" His question is overheard by Sir Piers Exton and is taken as an order. Exton rides to Yorkshire and murders Richard in Bolingbroke's name.

Bolingbroke is finally crowned king (Henry IV) but is consumed with guilt over his cousin Richard's murder and goes to the Holy Land on a pilgrimage of penance.

# Henry IV, Parts 1 and 2

Thought to be written immediately after Richard II, these two plays continue the royal saga of the newly crowned Henry IV, formerly known as Henry Bolingbroke.

*Part 1* features the first of three appearances by one of Shakespeare's best-loved characters, the carousing miscreant Falstaff (also in *Part 2* and *The Merry Wives of Windsor*), and illustrates the forging of the character of Prince Hal, later to become the much-admired Henry V.

## Part 1

King Henry IV is still consumed by guilt over the murder of his cousin Richard II and faces multiple rebellions. Henry cannot help but compare the valiant military commander Harry Hotspur, who has been fending off the Scots in the king's name, with his dissolute son Hal—who is more concerned with drinking with his gluttonous friend Sir John Falstaff.

Henry's admiration for Hotspur is short-lived, however, when the young nobleman turns against the king, suggesting that his brother-in-law Mortimer is the rightful heir to the throne. Hotspur takes up with the Welsh rebel Glendower (who has captured Mortimer) and Douglas, leader of the Scots.

Hal is scolded by his father, who suggests he is going down the same dissolute route as the former king Richard II and compares him unfairly to Hotspur, whom he considers to be more like himself ("Mars in swaddling clothing"). Hal vows to mend his ways and face Hotspur in battle at Shrewsbury, and commands Falstaff to lead a band of infantry.

The rebel camp is plagued with problems. Hotspur's father, the Earl of Northumberland, is too ill to join them and Glendower's forces are delayed. The king offers the hand of friendship, and go-between Worcester is dispatched to Hotspur's camp with talk of reconciliation. Instead, Worcester tells Hotspur to prepare for war.

Battle commences, and continues with heavy losses on both sides. The newly valiant Prince Hal is wounded but refuses to leave the fight, and ultimately kills Hotspur. Cowardly Falstaff decides it best to play dead, later finding Hotspur's body and presenting it to Prince Hal as his own kill. Claiming victory, Henry IV prepares for his next battle against Hotspur's father, Northumberland, and the absent Glendower.

## Part 2

Perhaps due to Falstaff's popularity from *Part 1*, Shakespeare gives the amoral drunkard a more central role in this later play, while Prince Hal is relatively absent from the drama. Of the two parts of the Henry IV story, this second part is often considered the weaker and is less frequently performed.

The action takes place over ten years between the battle of Shrewsbury in 1403 and Henry IV's death in 1413. His third son, Lancaster (aka John), successfully tricks the king's enemies in Yorkshire into laying down their arms and arrests them. Meanwhile, Falstaff ducks and dives in the Eastcheap tavern where he is faced with arrest for non-payment of debts. Eavesdropping at the tavern, Prince Hal hears Falstaff mocking him, and though the silver-tongued Falstaff seems to lie his way out of it, this event marks a turning point in their friendship. Hal is summoned to his father's deathbed and, mistaking the king's deep sleep for death, takes the crown from his chamber. Awaking to find his crown gone, Henry despairs of his heir's suitability to rule but is persuaded by his repentant son that England will be in safe hands, and then promptly dies.

At Hal's coronation as Henry V, Falstaff cheers loudly from the sidelines, hoping that his friend's high position will benefit him greatly. The new king spurns him, however. A changed character, Henry V promises to restore the fractured country to glory, and the play ends with Lancaster predicting that war with France is not far off.

For the next installment of the Henriad cycle, see *Henry V*, page 77.

# The Merry Wives of Windsor

Tradition has it that this play was written at the behest of Queen Elizabeth, who wanted to see her favorite character Falstaff *(Henry IV, Parts 1 and 2)* once more. This is Shakespeare's only comedy to take place in his native England, and notably features middle-class characters rather than royalty. Shakespeare has also chosen some particularly wonderful names for the characters, including Shallow, Slender, Quickly, Pistol, Nym, and Simple. These descriptive names would seem to be equally at home in the Wild West as in the no-less-ribald Globe Theatre.

## First half

Justice Shallow pursues the roguish Falstaff for payment of debts. Terminally short of cash, Falstaff decides to seduce two wealthy wives as a prelude to a little light extortion. He writes them identical love letters and dispatches his servants Nym and Pistol to deliver them to his targets, Mrs. Ford and Mrs. Page. The letters end up with the ladies' husbands instead.

Meanwhile, three men, Justice Shallow's cousin Abraham Slender, French physician Doctor Caius, and a young man called Fenton, are courting Anne Page—daughter of one of Falstaff's targets.

Mr. Page doesn't believe what Falstaff's letter implies, but Mr. Ford is suspicious. Disguising himself as "Master Brook," he offers Falstaff money to woo his wife, Mrs. Ford, on his behalf. Little do the men know that their wives are conspiring to teach them both a lesson.

## Second half

First they get Falstaff to hide in a laundry basket from the jealous Mr. Ford, then they dump him in the river. When he returns, this time rather bizarrely disguised as the "witch of Brainford," Falstaff is intercepted by Mr. Ford and thrashed. Finally, Mrs. Ford arranges to meet him at night in Windsor Forest. Disguised this time as Herne the Hunter, Falstaff is tormented by children dressed as fairies.

Also in the forest disguised as a fairy is Anne Page. She's meant to be eloping with Slender and also, through another arrangement, with Dr. Caius. However, she instead chooses the young Mr. Fenton. When they return married, her parents throw a celebratory party. All ends happily.

# Romeo and Juliet

Ah yes, this tale of teenage love gone horribly wrong is one of Shakespeare's most-performed and most-quoted plays, and has inspired countless ballets, operas, and movies. In fact, it is also one of his most filmed plays—racking up, according to the Internet Movie Database, an impressive sixty-plus productions and adaptations.

## First half

The story opens in Verona, where an unexplained "ancient grudge" divides the houses of rival aristocratic families the Montagues and the Capulets. In the first act we find members of each side insulting one another and generally brawling in the street. The Prince of Verona intercedes and lets it be known that any such further conduct may be punishable by death. By way of making peace, the head of the Capulet family, aka Old Capulet, invites the prince's relation Paris to dine with him and encourages him to court his young daughter Juliet, in the hope of cementing his ties to the prince.

Meanwhile, the hot-headed young Romeo Montague is interested in two things, stirring up trouble with the Capulets and wooing his beloved Rosaline. Knowing that she will be at a feast hosted by the Capulets to celebrate the union of Paris and Juliet, he and his friends decide to attend wearing masks.

At the feast, Romeo is instantly bewitched by Juliet and she by him. After a rather famous exchange involving a balcony and a variety of love-filled declarations, Romeo goes in search of the good-natured Friar Laurence, who agrees to officiate, and the young couple are quickly wed.

## Second half

Juliet's cousin Tybalt has challenged Romeo to a duel, which, given that they're now family, Romeo tries to prevent. But Romeo's friend Mercutio can't resist jeering at Tybalt, provoking the latter to wound him and flee. Mercutio's wound proves fatal, and an enraged Romeo murders Tybalt and consequently is banished from Verona.

All the while Juliet waits for her new husband to come for her, but in his place comes news of Tybalt's death and Romeo's exile. Not only that, but her oblivious father is still busy arranging her wedding with Paris.

By way of a solution, Friar Laurence convinces Romeo to flee to Mantua. He then advises Juliet to outwardly accept the union with Paris but then to drink a potion that will give the illusion that she is dead, at which point he would send word to Romeo to return for her. Juliet drinks the potion and "dies."

In Mantua, Friar Laurence's letter explaining Juliet's trick has gone astray and instead Romeo hears of Juliet's death. Grief-stricken, he goes to an apothecary to purchase poison, which he intends to drink once he has seen Juliet one final time.

At the Capulet tomb Romeo is challenged by Paris, so Romeo stabs him. Asking God (and Juliet) for forgiveness for the deaths of Paris and Tybalt, Romeo drinks his poison and dies.

Friar Laurence shows up just as Juliet is waking up, only to tell her of the deaths of both Paris and her beloved Romeo. Unable to face life without him, Juliet stabs herself with Romeo's knife and dies. Cheerful stuff.

At the play's conclusion the friar calls upon Old Capulet and Old Montague to look upon their dead children and see what their feud has amounted to, which is a bit rich considering his part in their deaths. The enemies embrace, but it's too little too late for the ill-fated "star cross'd lovers" Romeo and Juliet.

# Much Ado about Nothing

This much-loved comedy is built on three intertwining storylines. There's sibling rivalry between the virtuous Don Pedro and the evil Don John; the betrothal of Claudio and Hero (including false accusations of adultery and a faked death along the way); and the caustic love story of the wonderfully witty Beatrice and Benedick.

## First half

The play starts at the end of a battle between a prince, Don Pedro, and his half-brother, the illegitimate Don John. Post-battle, Don Pedro and his soldiers are welcomed to the estate of Leonato, governor of Messina. Don John, now reconciled with his brother is also invited to stay.

Among Don Pedro's soldiers are Claudio and Benedick. The former quickly falls for Leonato's daughter Hero, the latter swears off love entirely and has some memorably spiky exchanges with Leonato's adopted niece Beatrice on the subject.

Don John resents his brother's favorite, Claudio, and decides to sabotage his relationship with Hero. At a masked ball Don Pedro woos Hero for Claudio (as you do) but the devious Don John plants the notion in Claudio's mind that Don Pedro in fact wants her for himself. When this ploy fails, Don John gets his servant, Borachio, to seduce Hero's maid Margaret. Borachio then orchestrates a scenario where he woos Margaret, who is dressed as Hero, within sight of Claudio.

## Second half

This time Don John's scheme is successful, and Claudio believes that Hero has been unfaithful. He rejects her at their wedding, calling her a "rotten orange" among other names. Hero faints with the horror of it all, and Claudio and the other wedding guests leave. Even Hero's father Leonato has his doubts about her. Thankfully the officiating priest believes Hero to be virtuous and suggests they spread the word that, rather than just faint, she in fact died of grief at being falsely accused on her wedding day. The thinking being that the weight of her shock will prove her innocence and inspire guilt in her accusers.

Elsewhere, the town constable arrests Borachio when he hears him boasting of his deceit. Soon news of this arrest, and that Don John has fled, reaches Don Pedro and Claudio. Guilt-ridden, Claudio vows that in penance for Hero's death he will marry any woman of Leonato's choosing. The chosen female is a heretofore unseen niece, and, you guessed it, at the wedding this mysterious lady is revealed to be none other than Hero, back from the dead.

Meanwhile, Beatrice and Benedick have been tricked into believing that each is loved by the other and consequently discover true feelings of love. Beatrice still seems to have some doubts by the play's end, and the only way that Benedick can stop her outpouring of witticisms is with a kiss.

Everyone's happy, except maybe Don John, and they all dance happily at the wedding reception.

The plot is kick-started by a vicious slander leading to an apparent death. So clearly things are ado about *something*. The word *nothing* was Elizabethan slang for female genitalia; hence, in *Hamlet*, "nothing" is referred to as "a fair thought—to lie between maids' legs."

# *Henry V*

God for Harry, England and Saint George!" This play stirs nationalistic sentiment like no other—and you don't even have to be English to feel it. It marks the coming of age of Henry IV's once-dissolute and disappointing son "Hal," former drinking partner of Falstaff. The play covers the period between Henry's accession to the throne in 1413 and his marriage to Katherine of France in 1420.

We are guided through the play by the Chorus, who first asks the audience to use its imagination to transform the "wooden O" of the theater into the battlefield at Agincourt.

## First half

The play begins with the Archbishop of Canterbury and the Bishop of Ely discussing Henry's transformation of character from wild young man to wise king. We find the king himself weighing his lawful options to claim the throne of France. The archbishop urges him to pursue his hereditary claim through his great-great-grandmother. Henry is then insulted by the ambassador sent by the Dauphin, and the young king makes up his mind to wage war against the French.

Meanwhile, a plot against Henry's life is foiled, and from the Boar's Head Tavern we learn of the death of John Falstaff, everyone's favorite reprobate.

## Second half

And so to France, where the English first lay siege to Harfleur and then with weakened forces march on to Agincourt to face the army of the French king, which outnumbers the English five to one. Henry has to deliver a pretty rousing speech to convince his men to enter such a skewed battle, and he does: the Saint Crispin's Day speech ranks among Shakespeare's finest.

Against the odds the English are triumphant, suffering losses of twenty-eight to France's ten thousand. Obviously Shakespeare was being a little generous with the numbers, though

England's more sophisticated longbows did in reality give them an advantage.

Henry returns to England, and several years pass before he ventures to France again. In one of the play's most memorable scenes, Henry woos Princess Katherine in humorously incompetent Franglais. The two become engaged, and the rift between France and England is healed, temporarily at least.

In the play, the Dauphin insults Henry by offering him tennis balls—a jab at the king's perceived youth and inexperience. Although this may be an offering of Shakespeare's imagination, it was a real possibility. The game is thought to date back to the twelfth century.

## As You Like It

*"All the world's a stage,*
*And all the men and women merely players"*

Riddled with allusions to the theater and acting, this comedy could be described as experimental for its day. Caricature-like characters refer to themselves as players, and even the audience is encouraged to see itself as part of the act.

## First half

Duke Frederick has usurped the court of his older brother, Duke Senior, and has banished him and his daughter Rosalind to the Forest of Arden. Upset by her father's newfound tyranny, Frederick's daughter Celia heads off to the forest with Rosalind. Before Rosalind departs she falls in love with Orlando, who has been disenfranchised by his older brother Oliver. She then ventures into the forest disguised as a boy, Ganymede. Celia passes herself off as Aliena, Ganymede's sister, and Touchstone the clown accompanies them.

Meanwhile, Orlando is forced to flee the court when he learns of his wicked brother's intention to burn him in his bed, and he, too, ends up in the forest. He meets and is welcomed by Duke Senior, who seems to have taken enthusiastically to his new woodland home.

## Second half

Falsely believing Orlando to be involved in his daughter Celia's desertion, Duke Frederick orders Oliver to find him or lose his fortune. Orlando, however, is too busy hanging poems to Rosalind in the trees to worry. When Ganymede meets Orlando, "he" suggests that to cure his lovesickness Orlando should woo him as if he were Rosalind. At one point Aliena even ends up officiating at a mock wedding between Orlando and Rosalind-pretending-to-be-Ganymede-pretending-to-be-Rosalind!

In pursuit of his brother, Oliver ends up inadvertently being rescued by him. He is duly repentant and wants to give Orlando the family fortune in gratitude. He then finds time to fall in love with Aliena.

Seeing that the charade must come to an end, Ganymede promises to bring the real Rosalind to Orlando the next day. The reconciled couple are married, along with three other couples including Oliver and Aliena/Celia. The marriages are officiated over by Hymen (yes, really), the god of marriage.

This play features the biggest female role in Shakespeare. Rosalind speaks nearly 700 lines of dialogue—still fewer than Hamlet, who speaks more than 1,500.

## Julius Caesar

Caesar's story was a very popular subject in the 1580s, and it is likely that Shakespeare saw a few productions on the theme. Polonius refers to one such production in Hamlet. It is one of the best-loved and most-performed plays in Shakespeare's canon, and its account of Caesar's assassination has long since become the official version in popular imagination, though historians still argue many alternatives.

## First half

The play opens with Julius Caesar and his right-hand man
Mark Antony returning from a victorious battle against the
Roman general Pompey. Among the cheers, Caesar hears a
voice warning him to "beware the ides of March" (March
15th) and then receives a similar warning from a soothsayer—
both of which Caesar ignores.

The adoration of the Roman crowd leads Caius Cassius,
Marcus Brutus, and the senators of the Capitol to fear that the
people want Caesar to become their king and absolute ruler.
While Brutus is ambivalent, Cassius is quicker to express his
fears and to plot Caesar's downfall.

Brutus and Cassius collude to assassinate Caesar on his
next visit to the Capitol. On the eve of his visit, Caesar's wife,
Calpurnia, has a nightmare in which her husband is murdered,
and she forbids him to leave the house. Caesar chooses to
ignore this and various inauspicious signs, including a letter
from his supporter Artemidorus warning him against plotters.

## Second half

It is the ides of March, and a confident Caesar enters the Capitol, only to be set upon and stabbed by numerous assailants
and, finally, Brutus ("Et tu, Brute?"). After the murder, Brutus
faces the Roman crowd and tells them that they would have
become slaves under Caesar. Mark Antony then addresses them
and reminds them that Caesar three times refused the crown
of Rome and always shared his victories with the people. The

crowd are whipped into a vengeful frenzy and carry off the body of Caesar, their king. Cassius and Brutus flee and Mark Antony meets with Caesar's adopted son Octavius.

While preparing an army, the plotters Brutus and Cassius receive the news that one hundred senators have been put to death for their parts against Caesar and that the forces of Mark Antony and Octavius are marching to meet them at Philippi. That night, Brutus is haunted by the ghost of Julius Caesar. The following day the two sides meet in battle. When defeat seems likely Cassius falls on his own sword. When Brutus discovers Cassius's body, he asks his men to kill him, too. Finally Strato holds the sword for Brutus to fall upon. When Mark Antony hears of Brutus's death he says that Brutus acted honestly and with the common good in mind, and Octavius orders that his body be buried with respect.

*Antony and Cleopatra* picks up where this story left off: A new power struggle has replaced the previous one, and Mark Antony and Octavius find themselves on opposing sides (see page 115).

## Twelfth Night

In this play, also known as *What You Will,* Shakespeare again uses the plot device of twins separated by a storm at sea (see *The Comedy of Errors,* page 28). However, in this case Shakespeare adds a twist—the fated twins are brother and sister, Sebastian and Viola.

## First half

The setting is the fictional kingdom of Illyria, somewhere in the Adriatic Sea. Olivia, a rich countess, has vowed to mourn her brother's death for seven years and refuses to let Duke Orsino, or any other man for that matter, court her.

Meanwhile, a vicious storm has separated twins Sebastian and Viola, who has washed ashore in Illyria. Presuming her brother dead, Viola disguises herself as a young man named Cesario and finds work as Orsino's page. She quickly falls in love with him.

## Second half

Cesario is sent to Olivia to try to persuade her to hear Orsino's suit, but Olivia is much more interested in Cesario. Another of Olivia's wannabe suitors, the hard-drinking Sir Andrew Aguecheek, becomes jealous of Cesario and challenges him to a duel. The fight is broken up by the sudden appearance of Antonio, the captain of Viola's wrecked ship, who approaches her calling her "Sebastian." Elsewhere the real Sebastian is mistaken for Cesario. He's rather baffled by it all, though not as baffled as the "real" Cesario (aka Viola), especially when she is informed by a priest that she has just married Olivia. . . .

When brother and sister end up on stage at the same time, all becomes clear and they are joyfully reunited. Orsino proposes to Viola in a conclusion that is not quite as romantic as we might like—but at least she seems pleased. And Sebastian and Olivia confirm that they are now married, albeit not quite conventionally, but they also seem delighted nonetheless.

# Hamlet

Playing "the Dane" is a necessary test of greatness for any aspiring thespian, including Richard Burton, Kenneth Branagh, Sir Laurence Olivier, Sir Ian McKellen, and, of course, Sir John Gielgud. The renowned Sarah Bernhardt (1844–1923) was the first film Hamlet in 1900 and possibly the only Hamlet with a wooden leg. Hamlet is also the Bard's most filmed play. According to the Internet Movie Database, more than 160 films and adaptations of Hamlet have been made.

## Act One

"Something is rotten in the state of Denmark," and the ghost of the recently deceased Old King Hamlet stalks the battlements of the royal castle. At the urging of his friend Horatio, the grieving young Prince Hamlet goes to see the spirit and learns from it that the king died at the hands of his own brother, Claudius. This same brother has now not only installed himself on the Danish throne but in the bed of his brother's widow, Hamlet's mother Gertrude.

Hamlet promises the ghost that he will both remember and avenge him. But, gathering his thoughts, he wonders at the truth of what the spirit has told him.

## Act Two

Rather than confront the new king, the prince decides to adopt an "antic disposition"—feigning madness until he can find a way to coax a confession from his murderous uncle. The prince is self-aware enough to know that this ruse is a way of putting off revenge and chastises himself for it when he's alone, regularly.

Hamlet's mother and stepfather/uncle, however, initially take his strange new behavior for grief at his father's death—that is, until their long-winded, meddling, and morally dubious chief adviser, Polonius, informs them that he believes Hamlet to be in love with his daughter Ophelia.

## Act Three

The king and Polonius decide to use Ophelia as bait to draw out the truth about the change in Hamlet. It would seem, however, that there is in fact genuine feeling between the young couple. Hamlet has given Ophelia love letters and other tokens of his esteem, which, on her father Polonius's command, and with him and King Claudius watching from a hiding place, she returns to Hamlet. Hamlet viciously rebukes Ophelia and tells her "get thee to a nunnery." It's likely that Hamlet knows that they're being watched and mistakenly believes Ophelia to be in on the act.

Shortly thereafter, Hamlet comes up with an idea to scare a confession of murder from his uncle. A troupe of players are visiting the court, and Hamlet recruits them to perform a drama in which the player king is murdered and usurped by his brother, who claims both his throne and his wife. Claudius's response to the play is enough to confirm Hamlet's belief in his guilt, and the king flees the room for the chapel, where he prays alone for forgiveness for his crime. Hamlet comes upon him but again does not act, telling himself that to kill Claudius at prayer is to consign a killer's soul to heaven.

Instead, Hamlet turns his wrath on his mother and accuses her of complicity in his father's murder and of disgracing both her marriage vows and herself by marrying Claudius so soon. During this exchange, Polonius hides behind a wall hanging, and Hamlet, mistaking him for the king, stabs Polonius to death.

## Act Four

In the aftermath, Hamlet leaves for England with his old school friends Rosencrantz and Guildenstern. The trip is the brain-child of Claudius, who wants his nephew out of the way—permanently. The prince unwittingly carries with him letters commanding his own death.

With Hamlet dispatched, the court's attention is diverted to Ophelia, who has been driven mad upon the death of her father at the hands of her former beloved. Her brother Laertes vows revenge on Hamlet.

Meanwhile, Hamlet has been captured by pirates, his friends having continued to England. Having escaped the pirates, Hamlet writes to his friend Horatio that he is to meet him and learn a grave secret. . . . News of the prince's planned return reaches court, and Claudius and Laertes conspire to avenge the murder of Polonius. Queen Gertrude brings news that Ophelia has drowned herself in a moment of madness.

## Act Five

On their way back to court, Hamlet and Horatio walk through a churchyard where a gravedigger has just unearthed the skull of a former court jester. The prince picks up the skull and ponders the man's fate ("Alas, poor Yorick . . ."). The prince then learns that the grave they are digging is in fact for Ophelia. Hamlet and Ophelia's brother Laertes tussle by the graveside, and it is decided that they shall settle their dispute with a sword fight. Hamlet confides in Horatio that he found the letter ordering his death and replaced it with one ordering the deaths of Rosencrantz and Guildenstern.

At the duel of Hamlet and Laertes, King Claudius takes no chances. Not only has the tip of Laertes's sword been poisoned but he also has poisoned a chalice of wine for the prince to drink when he scores a hit. Queen Gertrude, however, toasts her son's first triumph over Laertes with the poisoned chalice and is killed. Hamlet is then wounded by Laertes, and they exchange swords in the confusion. Laertes, is wounded with his own poisoned blade. Knowing his fate, Laertes exposes Claudius's treachery, tells Hamlet of his imminent death, and begs for forgiveness. Hamlet then finally slays his uncle with the poisoned sword. With his dying breath, Hamlet asks Horatio to tell his story to others.

At the end of this revenge tragedy the stage has the expected body count the genre demands, but the play has delivered so much more than that. Shakespeare has taken a formulaic structure and turned it into one of the world's greatest, most thought-provoking works of art, littered with some of his very finest speeches—and the corpses of some of his most memorable characters.

Played in its entirety, the 4,024-line drama lasts for nearly five hours. The eponymous character alone speaks 1,506 lines. More often than not, the play is edited down to between two and three hours, but anyone who studied it at school will have read the full five glorious acts.

# "It was Greek to me"

# Common Quotes and Misquotes

Shakespeare's works are a close second to the Bible when it comes to being quoted—and are just as frequently misquoted, too. Here are some of the most common misquotes and misinterpretations of the Bard's words.

*Misinterpretation:* **"O, Romeo, Romeo . . . Wherefore art thou, Romeo?"**

—Juliet, *Romeo and Juliet*

This is a commonly misinterpreted quote, which tends to evoke an image of Juliet on her balcony calling out for her lover Romeo, i.e. "Where are you, Romeo?" But what it actually means is "*Why* are you Romeo?" as Juliet goes on to bemoan the fact that Romeo is a Montague and therefore a sworn enemy of her family, the Capulets.

*Misquote:* **"Alas, poor Yorick! I knew him well."**
*Original:* **"Alas, poor Yorick! I knew him, Horatio: a fellow of infinite jest, of most excellent fancy."**

—Prince Hamlet, *Hamlet*

This quote is paired with perhaps the most iconic of all theatrical images: the young, melancholy Prince Hamlet, musing on death with the skull of a jester in his hand. The addition of extra exclamation marks in other variations of this misquote might be attributable to the 1913 short silent comedy film starring Fatty Arbuckle, *Alas! Poor Yorick!*

*Misquote:* **"All that glitters is not gold."**
*Original:* **"All that glisters is not gold."**

—The Prince of Morocco, *The Merchant of Venice*

This misquote is a commonly used phrase that warns its recipient not to be misled by show. The change from glister to glitter is straightforward enough—the former was already a bit archaic even in Shakespeare's day. J. R. R. Tolkien changed the quote further still in *The Lord of the Rings* to "All that is gold does not glitter."

*Misquote:* **"Gild the lily."**
*Original:* **"To gild refined gold, to paint the lily"**

—Salisbury, *King John*

Now a phrase in common use, "gilding the lily" is synonymous with over-embellishment.

*Misquote:* **"Lead on, Macduff."**
*Original:* **"Lay on, Macduff, and damned be him who first cries 'Hold, enough!'"**

—Macbeth, *Macbeth*

The misquote here suggests that Macbeth wants Macduff to begin moving in to fight, or to lead the way. The original, however, is a call to immediate action. Also, Macduff's "One fell swoop" is often quoted as "One foul swoop."

*Misquote:* **"Methinks the lady doth protest too much."**
*Original:* **"The lady doth protest too much, methinks."**

—Queen Gertrude, *Hamlet*

This is one of the most commonly heard misquotes of Shakespeare and has, over time, taken on a quite different meaning to the original. The word *protest* in its original context means "vow." In her dry appraisal of the play that Hamlet has staged to prick her conscience, Gertrude fails to see the irony that the onstage queen is a much more dedicated wife to her first husband than she herself ever was to the old King Hamlet. Gertrude believes the queen overdoes the promises to her husband. With time *protest* has come to be defined as "to deny" or "object"—the implication being that the more a lady objects, the more likely it is that her objections are in fact a pretense.

It wasn't until the seventeenth century that women appeared on the stage; before this, young boys often played the roles of women in William Shakespeare's plays. Nevertheless, women still had dominant supporting roles in many of his works. Cleverly, unbeknownst to the men, many of the women actually were made to be more authoritative than the men and generally controlled the actions of the play.

Three such plays with powerful women are *Macbeth, Hamlet,* and *King Lear.* Lady Macbeth advises and assists her husband in killing the king so he will obtain the throne; in *Hamlet,* Gertrude and Ophelia are the two loves of the main character; and in *King Lear* three women have the ability to drive the king mad.

"The rest is science" is another well-known phrase, which many believe came from Hamlet's final words "The rest is silence." Ironically, the meaning behind Hamlet's words isn't pure science; some believe it to mean that Hamlet faces the final truth that there is in fact nothing after death but emptiness, while others believe that Hamlet will finally be at peace and that with his death, no more pain will be able to enter his ears. His death, in other words, will be his eternal silence and he will finally have an undisturbed rest.

Hamlet is Shakespeare's longest play and among the most powerful and influential tragedies. It became one of his most popular works and ... well, the rest is history.

*Misinterpretation:* **"Now is the winter of our discontent."**
*Original:* **"Now is the winter of our discontent/**
**Made glorious summer by this sun of York."**
—Richard, Duke of Gloucester, *Richard III*

This is not so much a misquote as it is a misinterpretation that ultimately delivers the opposite of the original intended meaning. In the absence of the second half of the line, the meaning suggests that the discontent is happening now, rather than the fact that the metaphorical winter referred to has been banished by this sun [son] of York—meaning Richard, Duke of Gloucester—soon to be King Richard III.

*Misquote:* **"Bubble bubble, toil and trouble."**
*Original:* **"Double, double toil and trouble."**

—The weird sisters, *Macbeth*

The sisters (aka the three witches) are asking for double the toil and trouble as they brew up hideous potions in their cauldron. The misquote "Bubble bubble" provides an evocative shorthand, conjuring as it does the bubbling cauldron full of frogs, snakes, cats, bats, and rats.

*Misquote:* **"Discretion is the better part of valour."**
*Original:* **"The better part of valor is discretion,**
  **(in the which better part I have saved my life.)"**

—Falstaff, *Henry IV, Part I*

The essential meaning of this misquote is true to the original. Shakespeare's much-loved character Falstaff muses on the benefits of caution and thinking before one acts.

*Misattribution:* **"Friends, Romans, countrymen, lend me your ears"**

—Mark Antony, *Julius Caesar*

The quote is right but the attribution is often wrong. It is often presumed that this line is spoken by Julius Caesar, but in fact it is uttered by Mark Antony at Julius Caesar's funeral.

*Misquote:* **"A rose by any other name smells just as sweet."**
*Original:* **"What's in a name? That which we call a rose by any other word would smell as sweet."**

—Juliet, *Romeo and Juliet*

The meaning of the misquote here is much the same as the original. The young couple Romeo and Juliet are divided by their respective surnames Montague and Capulet and the bitter feud between their families. Juliet chooses to love the boy behind the name. It has also been suggested that this line is an in-joke about Shakespeare's rival Rose Theatre, a place with notoriously unsophisticated sanitary arrangements. The first part of the original line "What's in a name?" is itself frequently and correctly quoted.

*Misquote:* "To the manor born"
*Original:* "But to my mind, though I am native here /
And to the manner born, it is a custom/More honour'd
in the breach than the observance."

—Prince Hamlet, *Hamlet*

The misquote refers to being born into nobility Hamlet's meaning is broader and refers to Danish custom. The misquote got an extra stamp of legitimacy when it was used as the title of the popular late-1970s British television sitcom *To the Manor Born*.

# "A kingdom for a stage"

# Shakespeare's Plays 1603–1606

This was the period of Shakespeare's great tragedies, which included *Othello, King Lear,* and *Macbeth*.

## *Troilus and Cressida*

This story has about as rich a lineage as any can have. Its sources include Homer's epic poem *The Iliad* and Chaucer's almost-as-epic *Troilus and Criseyde*, as well as William "printing press" Caxton's *The Recuyell of the Histories of Troy*.

Shakespeare uses these sources to create his own unique meditation on love (and jealousy) and war, crossing every genre on the way. The play includes elements of farce, romance, comedy, tragedy, the heroic, and, ultimately, satire.

### First half

The action takes place in Troy against a backdrop of the long war between the Trojans and the Greeks. Helen (yes, *that* Helen), queen of Sparta, has been "abducted" by her lover Paris, prince of Troy. Her husband, King Menelaus, along with his brother Agamemnon, is leading the Greeks in a rather lengthy rescue attempt—they've besieged Troy for ten years already, and everyone's getting a bit testy. Also in the Greek camp are some familiar names from classics studies—Ajax, Achilles, and Ulysses (aka Odysseus from Homer's *Odyssey*).

The war side of the story is concerned with the futility of the battle between Trojans and Greeks and the egos of the warriors involved. The love story is between the eponymous Trojans, Troilus and Cressida. But don't be fooled by the title and the fact that they are from opposing families—Romeo and Juliet (see page 73) they ain't.

Troilus is madly in love with Cressida, and while she gives the impression of liking him rather a lot, too, her head is easily turned. On her way to the Greek camp, and at the behest of her turncoat father Calchus, Cressida falls in love with her escort, Diomedes.

## Second half

Troilus goes to find his love, but on his way meets Ulysses, who arranges for Troilus to overhear the couple courting. Troilus flies into a rage and rampages through the Greek camp, sparking a full-scale battle in which his eldest brother Hector is killed and the great and proud Achilles is shown to be dishonorable on the battlefield.

The play ends on rather a low note. The war continues as hopelessly as before, and love, sadly, does not triumph.

# Othello

This tragic tale of deception and jealousy is perhaps Shake-speare's most heartbreaking play.

## First half

The action begins when Othello, a Moor who has risen to the rank of general in the Venetian army, chooses Cassio as his lieutenant over his ensign, Iago. Believing himself wronged, the relentlessly vengeful Iago pursues a cunning plot to bring about Othello's downfall.

First he informs the Venetian senator Brabantio that his daughter Desdemona has eloped with Othello. When Othello is brought before the court, however, he speaks eloquently of his innocent love for Desdemona and how she in turn came to love him. Brabantio decides to allow the marriage, albeit reluctantly.

With a Turkish invasion of Cyprus coming, Othello heads up an army to defend the island and takes his new wife along with him. There, Iago gets his perceived usurper Cassio drunk and orchestrates a brawl, which results in the new lieutenant being stripped of his rank by Othello. Iago then suggests to Cassio that he petition Othello—via Desdemona—to reinstate him. Meanwhile, he begins insinuating to Othello that Desdemona has more than a passing interest in Cassio.

Iago then acquires a handkerchief given to Desdemona by Othello and plants it in Cassio's quarters. Cassio in turn finds it and gives it to his lover Bianca. When Othello questions Desdemona as to the whereabouts of the handkerchief, she answers innocently that she does not know. The seeds of suspicion are sown, but Iago leaves nothing to chance and arranges for Othello to overhear Cassio talking about his affair with Desdemona, though in reality Bianca is the true subject of their conversation. Blinded by rage at Cassio and Desdemona's betrayal, Othello orders Iago to murder Cassio and reports that he will dispatch with his wife himself.

## Second half

Venetian envoys arrive and are horrified to witness Othello's public treatment of his wife as he insults and then strikes her. Rather than carry out the dirty deed himself, Iago persuades Roderigo, who is in love with Desdemona, to challenge and kill Cassio. Roderigo is unsuccessful, and Iago murders him to keep him silent.

Meanwhile, Othello is alone with Desdemona, whom he accuses of infidelity. She protests and protests, but the "green ey'd monster"—jealousy—has turned him from an honorable man into a murderer and he smothers his innocent young wife with a pillow. When Desdemona's maidservant Emilia (Iago's wife) discovers the body, she reveals that the handkerchief found its way into Cassio's possession via Iago, who asked her to take it from her mistress. Iago stabs his wife and flees. Realizing Desdemona's innocence and his own guilt, Othello commits suicide in front of the Venetian envoys. Iago is captured and taken to Venice to be punished and Cassio is named governor of Cyprus.

# *Measure for Measure*

This play is a hard one to categorize, which is why it is classed as one of Shakespeare's "problem plays," alongside *All's Well That Ends Well* (see page 112) and *Troilus and Cressida* (see page 102). While the play is essentially a comedy, its central concerns are quite weighty.

## First half

The Duke of Vienna, a thoroughly nice but inept ruler, allows many of the city's young women to fall under the sway of lusty young men and thus into disrepute. Many young couples are living together unwed—an act prohibited by law and punishable by death, for the male party at least. However the duke will not enforce it for fear of falling from favor. Seeing that something must finally be done, the duke absents himself and appoints the saintly Angelo to take over the city and bring back its lost morality.

The duke pretends to go to Poland, but actually remains in Vienna disguised as a friar to watch Angelo's work for himself. First on his deputy's hit list is Claudio, a young man imprisoned and sentenced to death by beheading for seducing a young lady away from her family. Claudio's convent-bound sister Isabella is talked into seducing and thereby mollifying Angelo. She quickly discovers that it won't take much flirting to corrupt the once-saintly Angelo with lust.

## Second half

Disguised as a friar, the duke eavesdrops on Claudio and Isabella. She hesitantly reveals that her virginity can be used to buy her brother's life from Angelo. Claudio pushes her to do it but she refuses, cursing her brother to "Die, perish." The duke approaches Isabella with an alternative plan: she should accept Angelo's offer but then allow Mariana, a woman once rejected by Angelo, to replace her in Angelo's bed. Mariana is keen on the idea as she believes that sleeping with Angelo will reconfirm the engagement he once reneged on.

The plan works, but at dawn a message comes from the treacherous Angelo to execute Claudio anyway and to send his head as proof. As it happens there's a head going spare at the jail—that of a pirate who just died of fever and looks uncannily like Claudio—and this is sent to Angelo instead.

The duke announces his "return" to Vienna. Isabella and Mariana confront Angelo who denies everything, but the duke can, of course, confirm their story. Angelo is ordered to marry Mariana . . . and then be executed. He is pardoned when his new wife pleads for his life. Claudio is presented alive and well to the joy of his sister and can now marry his pregnant girlfriend Juliet. The duke proposes to Isabella, but we don't get to hear her answer so you can pick your own ending, the convent or marriage. I like to think she chose the former over the meddling duke.

The subject matter of *Measure for Measure* is close to the bone for Shakespeare. We know that his own wife was pregnant when he married her, and there's some question as to whether he entered the union willingly.

# King Lear

Based on the legend of Leir, the semi-mythological Celtic king of the Britons, this unforgiving tragedy comes in two versions. The first appeared in quarto form in 1608 as *The True Chronicle of the History of King Lear and His Three Daughters* and the second in the First Folio of 1623 as *The Tragedy of King Lear*. The two versions are usually combined in performance.

## Act One

Desiring a tranquil retirement, old King Lear decides to divide up his kingdom between his three daughters Goneril, Regan, and Cordelia, and to live with each one on rotation. However, his method is flawed and pits the sisters against each other: he will divide his property according to who loves him most. Regan and Goneril take the sycophantic approach and lavish false esteem upon their aged father, while the sincere and honest Cordelia cannot bring herself to behave in such a fawning way and is punished with disinheritance by her hot-headed father. Lear also banishes his loyal supporter Kent for questioning this action.

With Cordelia married off to the king of France, Goneril and Regan share rule over the country. It's not long before the sisters decide that something must be done about their elderly father.

## Act Two

Lear is staying in the palace of Goneril's husband, Albany, with a retinue of one hundred knights. Goneril decides that Lear's knights are getting too rowdy and tells her father that he must reduce their number to fifty. Disgusted by his daughter's ingratitude, Lear leaves the palace. In the interim, the banished Kent has returned disguised as "Caius," and he becomes Lear's servant.

Elsewhere, the Earl of Gloucester's illegitimate son Edmund seeks to disenfranchise his legitimate brother Edgar, even though their father claims to love both sons equally. Edmund gives his father a forged letter in which Edgar supposedly states his intention to seize all the family estates. He then fools his father into thinking that Edgar plans to kill him. Edgar flees, and stays close to his father's castle disguising himself as "Poor Tom," a lunatic beggar. Regan and her husband Cornwall arrive at Gloucester's castle, as does Lear's servant Caius. Caius confronts Goneril's lackey and go-between Oswald, and Cornwall punishes Caius by putting him in the stocks. When Lear arrives, he finds his loyal servant still in the stocks, and his own position severely diminished. Regan refuses to see him unless he admits that he has wronged Goneril. Lear refuses to do so and is then told by Regan that he must reduce his retinue to twenty-five men.

Goneril arrives on the scene and Lear decides to go with her, as he can at least have fifty men at her castle, but she asks him why he needs any at all. Enraged by their treatment of him, Lear leaves the castle cursing his daughters and heads out into a storm. As a final insult the daughters suggest that Gloucester lock his doors against the king's return to teach him a lesson.

## Act Three

Gloucester has received a letter informing him that forces from France are coming to help restore Lear's power. He foolishly shares this information with Edmund, and heads into the storm.

He finds the king teetering on the brink of madness, and brings him to the shelter of a farmhouse where they meet the disguised Edgar. There he explains to Lear that Goneril and Regan are planning to do away with him but that he'll find safety at the French camp in Dover.

Within the castle, Edmund has shown Gloucester's letter to Cornwall. When Gloucester returns Regan and Cornwall interrogate him, pluck out his eyes, and throw him out of his own home. Both sisters then turn their attentions to the devious Edmund and vie for his affections.

## Acts Four & Five

Lear and Cordelia reunite, and he begs forgiveness. But as war breaks out between England and France, we learn that they have been captured, and Edmund gives orders for them to be murdered. We then learn that Goneril has poisoned Regan and stabbed herself to death.

Arrested by Goneril's relatively honorable husband Albany, and confronted by his brother Edgar, Edmund repents and urges haste in calling off the executions of Lear and Cordelia. It is too late and King Lear enters carrying the corpse of his daughter. Albany announces that all power is restored to the king—a pronouncement that is also too late. The king has lost his mind entirely and dies of grief. Albany and Edgar are left to rule.

All known accounts of the Lear story before Shakespeare have happy endings. Lear and Cordelia are ultimately reunited and survive. But Shakespeare was true to the tragedy model and kills both father and daughter off. However, the happy ending made a comeback when it was subjected to what is known as "Tatification," after Irish author Nahum Tate (1652–1715). Tate rewrote the play to give it a happier ending. In his version Cordelia marries Edgar, Lear survives, and his three daughters are reunited. This version of the play was performed for some 150 years.

# All's Well That Ends Well

Set in France, this play tells the story of a young woman's tireless quest to get her man. It is one of Shakespeare's least-performed works, and there are no records of it being performed during his lifetime.

## First half

Helena, a ward of the Countess of Roussillon, is head over heels in love with the countess's son Bertram, a snobbish young man who definitely does not return her sentiments.

Helena's father, a physician, has died, but Helena carries on his medical legacy and saves the life of the king of France. In gratitude, the king grants Helena's wish and compels Bertram to marry her. But immediately after the wedding her new husband absconds to Italy under the pretext of going to war. From there, he sends her a letter stating that he will not consider her to be his wife until she manages to get his ring on her finger and becomes pregnant with his child.

## Second half

The determined Helena makes her way to Florence in pursuit of Bertram, but there finds that he is busy trying to seduce Diana, the daughter of the house where he lodges. Diana and Helena hatch a scheme to reunite the wedded couple, with Helena taking Diana's place in her bed for a night with the oblivious Bertram, and getting the prized ring in the process

(Shakespeare was fond of this bed-switching trick; see *Measure for Measure*, page 106).

False news that Helena has died in France reaches Bertram, and he decides the coast is clear to return home and woo a more suitable bride, the daughter of Lord Lafeu. However, when Helena shows up sporting his ring and a pregnant belly, Bertram has no choice but to accept her as his wife. Helena is delighted with herself.

# Macbeth

Though today Macbeth is a staple in theaters and on school and university curriculum, this play is reputed to carry a curse. Nobody is sure where it originates from, but actors to this day believe it is bad luck to speak the name of the play. Often euphemistically referred to as "The Scottish Play," productions of Macbeth have been known to go horribly wrong, dating right back to the very first performance, when the boy playing Lady Macbeth died backstage.

In a 1942 production featuring John Gielgud, three actors died (Duncan plus two witches), and the set designer killed himself. The highest number of *Macbeth*-related fatalities, however, occurred in New York in 1848 when rival actors William Charles Macready of England and America's Edwin Forrest staged simultaneous, competing productions that led to a riot in which more than twenty people died. The play itself is no less bloody and tragic.

## First half

Macbeth and his fellow-general Banquo are returning to Scotland after quelling a Norwegian rebellion against King Duncan. They meet three witches on the road who foretell that Macbeth will be appointed Thane of Cawdor and then king of Scotland. They also tell Banquo that one day his sons will rule.

As a reward for his bravery, King Duncan does indeed bestow the title of thane of Cawdor upon Macbeth. When the new thane tells his wife of the prophesy and how it seems to be unfolding, she cajoles him into murdering King Duncan, who is their guest, to speed up her husband's journey to the throne. Though the king's sons escape from Macbeth's castle, they are blamed for the murder, and the way is clear for the murderer to be declared king.

Remembering the rest of the prophesy, about Banquo's sons ruling the country, Macbeth sends assassins to kill them. Though Banquo is killed, his son Fleance escapes. On the very same day, a terrified Macbeth is haunted by the ghost of Banquo. He goes to the witches for guidance, and they tell him that "no man born of woman" will ever murder him.

## Second half

When Macbeth hears that Macduff, thane of Fife, has fled to England in an act of defiance, the new king orders that Lady Macduff and her children be killed. Macduff and Malcolm, son of the murdered Duncan, plot a revolt against their murderous new king.

Though it was she who encouraged her husband's corruption and the murder of King Duncan, Lady Macbeth is consumed by guilt to the point of madness, and she takes her own life.

Feeling safeguarded by the witches' prophesy that "no man born of woman" will kill him, Macbeth meets Macduff in single combat. But upon learning that Macduff was born by Caesarean section rather than naturally, Macbeth sees his sins and his fate and surrenders to his execution at the hands of the man he has so wronged. Malcolm is crowned king.

History buffs will know that the final part of the prophesy comes true later: Banquo's descendants will one day rule in the form of King James I, the reigning monarch at the time the play was first performed.

If you do happen to say the word *Macbeth* within earshot of an actor, quoting Hamlet's "Angels and ministers of grace defend us!" is thought to counter the curse's effect.

## Antony and Cleopatra

This play begins in 40 B.C., four years after the death of Julius Caesar (see page 81).

## First half

Mark Antony shares the rule of Rome with Lepidus and the former emperor's nephew Octavius, but their power is threatened by Pompey, son of Julius Caesar's former rival, Pompey the Great.

Antony, however, is in Alexandria, consumed by his love for the charismatic but capricious Cleopatra, Queen of Egypt and former mistress of both Caesar and Pompey the Great. When a confusion of news reaches him about his wife Fulvia and his brother challenging Octavius, then that Fulvia is in fact dead and the younger Pompey has declared his intention to avenge his father's death, Antony returns to Rome.

In Rome, Lepidus and Octavius discuss Antony's newfound decadence and how they need his help to see off Pompey's advancing navy. When Antony arrives he and Octavius make peace and to seal the deal Antony marries Octavius's unimaginatively named sister Octavia. Upon receiving this piece of news in the East, Cleopatra threatens its bearer with a knife.

## Second half

The flimsy peace does not last long. Octavius denounces Antony in the Senate and imprisons Lepidus for treachery. When Pompey is killed, Octavius is closer than ever to absolute power. He is therefore outraged to learn that Antony has named Cleopatra queen of a swathe of Eastern territories. War is inevitable.

As Antony prepares to fight Octavius's superior fleet at sea, Cleopatra sends sixty ships to support him. However, when her ships retreat, Antony is forced to follow. Antony then petitions Octavius to acknowledge Cleopatra as queen and allow him to live in Egypt. But Octavius agrees only to the first part and asks Cleopatra to drive Antony out of Egypt. Antony sees no option but to engage Octavius in battle.

When Cleopatra's ships let him down again, a furious Antony is forced to retreat. In fear of her life, Cleopatra hides in her family tomb and sends out word that she has killed herself. Heartbroken and defeated, the old warrior Antony falls on his sword. Before he dies Antony hears that Cleopatra lives still and asks to be brought to her. She begs forgiveness, and he dies in her arms.

Cleopatra is seized by Octavius's soldiers. Knowing that Octavius intends to parade her around like a trophy, the queen kills herself using poisonous snakes. Moved by her death, Octavius orders that the famous lovers be buried side by side.

# Coriolanus

This is one of Shakespeare's longest plays and certainly his most political. It is also the Bard's least-performed tragedy, possibly because its central character is rather unsympathetic.

## First half

The action takes place in ancient Rome, where food shortages cause rioting in the street, and the Senate struggles to meet the demands of the commoners. On top of this, Rome is under attack by the Volsces, led by Aufidius. Caius Martius, a military hero who openly despises the ordinary citizens of Rome and mocks their representatives, is called upon to fend them off.

Following his glorious defeat of the Volscian army, Martius is renamed Coriolanus, in reference to Corioli, the location of the battle. Despite his unpopularity, it is proposed that Coriolanus be named consul. However the tribunes representing the people of Rome, Brutus and Sicinius, prevent this happening by reminding him that he must appear humble before the plebeians—the commoners he hates so much. Coriolanus struggles to appear humble and ultimately snaps, saying he would rather die than seek public approval. He is banished from Rome, the place he has saved from its enemies many times over.

## Second half

Set on revenge, Coriolanus disguises himself as a beggar and gains access to the house of his old foe Aufidius, leader of the Volscian army. He reveals himself, acknowledges the damage he has done in the past, and offers his services against the Romans. Aufidius accepts and they advance on Rome. As they near the city, Aufidius finds himself plagued with jealousy at Coriolanus's military prowess.

Meanwhile Coriolanus's former Roman allies appeal to him to stop his advance on Rome to no avail. But when the warrior's wife, mother, and son make a similar appeal, he is forced to listen. Aufidius praises Coriolanus's mercy while scheming to exploit his about-turn. When they return to Antium to face the Volscian elders, the duplicitous Aufidius accuses Coriolanus of breaking his oath to them. With the backing of the crowd rather than the elders, Aufidius and his henchmen murder Coriolanus. Shortly thereafter Aufidius is consumed with remorse and states that the Roman Coriolanus shall have a "noble memory."

Democracy (embodied in the play by the malleable will of the common people) is put in opposition to autocracy (embodied by the rigid, self-righteous Coriolanus), but Shakespeare offers no conclusion as to which provides a "better" political system—instead the audience is left with much to muse upon.

# "Love is blind"

# Shakespeare's Sonnets and Other Poems

L ove sonnets were all the rage in the 1590s, and Shake-speare tapped into the trend with great success—although a rather large question mark still looms over whether he gave permission for his sonnets to be published at all. Shakespeare's poems express love and life humbly, realistically and, above all, believably. They are also inadvertently the source of some of the literary world's greatest intrigues, spawning dozens of theories about Shakespeare's love life, marriage, and sexuality.

## The Sonnets

Shakespeare's 154 sonnets are sometimes named by their open-ing line, but more usually by the order they appeared when first published in 1609. Sonnets 1 to 126 are addressed to a young man, often referred to as the "Fair Youth." The first seventeen are known as the "procreation" sonnets, as the poet urges the young man to marry and have children so that his beauty will be passed to his children.

Lines within the Fair Youth poems appear to express the poet's love for the young man and at times to chastise him for his love for a rival poet. As a consequence, there has been much speculation about Shakespeare's sexuality. The dedication page of the first edition of the sonnets has been used by some to try to substantiate claims that Shakespeare was homosexual, and to identify the object of this affection as a Mr. W. H. The title page reads:

TO.THE.ONLIE.BEGETTER.OF.THESE.INSUING.
SONNETS.Mr.W.H.ALL. HAPPINESSE.AND.THAT.
ETERNITIE.PROMISED.BY.OUR.EVER-LIVING.
POET.
  WISHETH.THE.WELL-WISHING.ADVENTURER.
IN.SETTING.FORTH.TT

The author of the dedication, "TT," is usually identified as the sonnets' publisher, Thomas Thorpe. That the dedication was not written by Shakespeare does not deter speculation about the identity of, and Shakespeare's relationship with, the mysterious Mr. W. H.

One of the likelier W. H. candidates put forth is William Herbert, earl of Pembroke. The posthumously published First Folio of 1623 is, after all, dedicated to him. The primary problem with the earl claim is that it would be quite unusual to address an aristocrat as *Mr.* Another W. H. candidate is Henry Wriothesley, earl of Southampton, to whom *Venus and Adonis* and *The Rape of Lucrece* were dedicated by Shakespeare himself. But why the reversed initials? And why call him "Mr." when he, too, was an earl?

That the dedication refers to Mr. W. H. as the "begetter" of the poems, i.e. their author, opens another can of worms. We're then in the murky territory of conspiracy theories about who "really" wrote Shakespeare (see introduction, page 8).

The philosopher Bertrand Russell and Shakespeare scholar Jonathan Bate both suggest that W. H. is simply a typesetting error—that it should have read "W. S.," i.e. William Shakespeare, or "W. Sh." This is my preferred solution to the "problems" posed by the dedication, if the most mundane.

## The Dark Lady

The theory that Shakespeare was gay takes a knock in the last section of the sonnets, which are addressed to the poet's *mistress*. The woman who appears from Sonnet 127 on is usually referred to as the Dark Lady, because of her hair color and complexion as described by the poet:

*If snow be white, why then her breasts are dun;*
*If hairs be wires, black wires grow on her head* (130)

*Then I swear beauty herself is black,*
*And all they foul that thy complexion lack* (132)

Candidates for the Dark Lady include Mary Fitton, a lady-in-waiting at Elizabeth's court; Emilia Bassano Lanier, mistress of Shakespeare's company patron; the wife of close friend John Davenant, whose son William later claimed to be Shakespeare's illegitimate son; and the wife of John Florio, the secretary to Shakespeare's one-time patron. Shakespeare's wife Anne usually appears far down the list.

## No. 130

*My mistress' eyes are nothing like the sun;*

*Coral is far more red, than her lips red:*

*If snow be white, why then her breasts are dun;*

*If hairs be wires, black wires grow on her head.*

*I have seen roses damasked, red and white,*

*But no such roses see I in her cheeks;*

*And in some perfumes is there more delight*

*Than in the breath that from my mistress reeks.*

*I love to hear her speak, yet well I know*

*That music hath a far more pleasing sound;*

*I grant I never saw a goddess go;*

*My mistress, when she walks, treads on the ground.*

*And yet by heaven, I think my love as rare*

*As any she belied with false compare.*

## Iambic pentameter

As you'll no doubt remember from school, the majority of the sonnets are constructed in three 4-line stanzas called quatrains and a final couplet, following the rhyme scheme abab cdcd efef gg. They are written in iambic pentameter, the same meter used in the plays.

These two words strike fear into the heart of many a former student of the Bard, but really it's just a fancy way of referring to the rhythm of Shakespeare's poetry, how many beats or "feet" (units of rhythm) there are in a line. A foot is made up of two syllables, one of which bears the emphasis when spoken aloud. Shakespeare used this meter to make the language natural-sounding and easy to speak—and because it was in vogue at the time. Lines in iambic pentameter have ten syllables and therefore five beats/feet, following the pattern weak-STRONG.

If we look at the opening line of Shakespeare's most famous sonnet, "No. 18," we see the weak-STRONG pattern in action:

| Syllable: | 1 | **2** | 3 | **4** | 5 | **6** | 7 | **8** | 9 | **10** |
|---|---|---|---|---|---|---|---|---|---|---|
| | da-DUM | | da-DUM | | da-DUM | | da-DUM | | da-DUM | |
| | Shall **I** | | com**pare** | | thee **to** | | a **sum**mer's | | **day**? | |

Take a sampling of Shakespeare's verse from the sonnets and plays and you'll see that, with few exceptions, the same rule applies across the board.

## No. 18

Shall I compare thee to a summer's day?
Thou art more lovely and more temperate;
Rough winds do shake the darling buds of May,
And summer's lease hath all too short a date;
Sometime too hot the eye of heaven shines,
And often is his gold complexion dimm'd;
And every fair from fair sometime declines,
By chance or nature's changing course untrimm'd;
But thy eternal summer shall not fade,
Nor lose possession of that fair thou ow'st;
Nor shall Death brag thou wander'st in his shade,
When in eternal lines to time thou grow'st:
So long as men can breathe or eyes can see,
So long lives this, and this gives life to thee.

# *Other Poems*

Shakespeare published two longer poems, *Venus and Adonis* and *The Rape of Lucrece*, during a period when playhouses were closed because of the plague (1593–4). Both were very popular in their day but do not have the broader appeal of the sonnets for a contemporary audience. Another poem, *A Lover's Complaint*, was appended to the first edition of Shakespeare's sonnets in 1609, but its authorship is hotly contended. It is written in the same rhyme royal style as *The Rape of Lucrece*, but because of the relatively poor quality of this poem and the presence of incongruously un-Shakespearian language within it, it is often excluded from the canon and treated with suspicion.

There are also some distinct poems within plays such as *Love's Labour's Lost* and *Romeo and Juliet*. The latter play begins with a sonnet in the prologue, and the first conversation between the eponymous lovers is in fact a sonnet in duet (act I, scene 5). Romeo speaks the first four lines, then Juliet has four. They share the next four and the final couplet, and then comes the crowning glory. After a few more words in verse are exchanged, they share their first kiss.

**ROMEO**

*If I profane with my unworthiest hand*
*This holy shrine, the gentle sin is this:*
*My lips, two blushing pilgrims, ready stand*
*To smooth that rough touch with a tender kiss.*

**JULIET**

*Good pilgrim, you do wrong your hand too much,*
*Which mannerly devotion shows in this;*
*For saints have hands that pilgrims' hands do touch,*
*And palm to palm is holy palmers' kiss.*

**ROMEO**

*Have not saints lips, and holy palmers too?*

**JULIET**

*Ay, pilgrim, lips that they must use in prayer.*

**ROMEO**

*O, then, dear saint, let lips do what hands do;*
*They pray, grant thou, lest faith turn to despair.*

**JULIET**

*Saints do not move, though grant for prayers' sake.*

**ROMEO**

*Then move not, while my prayer's effect I take.*

# "Our revels are now ended"

# Shakespeare's Plays 1607–1613

During this time Shakespeare began to collaborate with other playwrights, who greatly influenced his work. With the help of John Fletcher, the tragicomedy—also known as the romance—was born. Like comedy, romance includes a love intrigue and has a happy ending. And like tragedy, romance addresses some serious, dark themes, like betrayal. Four of the Bards most well known romances are *Pericles, Cymbeline, The Winter's Tale*, and *The Tempest*.

## Pericles (with George Wilkins)

Blending tragedy with comedy, and allegory with fairy-tale magic, this play is considered to be Shakespeare's first romance. Others in this genre include *The Tempest* (see page 138) and *The Winter's Tale* (see page 136).

These plays are presented as ancient tales being retold for the audience's entertainment. This gives the playwright much license to be as fantastical and unbelievable as he wants. In *Pericles* the story of the play is told to us by John Gower, the fourteenth-century English poet, who presides over events and acts as Chorus throughout, thus ensuring that the audience is reminded at frequent intervals that this is just a story.

There is some support for the idea that this play was written in collaboration with the dramatist and pamphleteer George Wilkins, who was associated with Shakespeare's theatrical company, the King's Men. Wilkins published a novel in 1608, the same year in which it is assumed *Pericles* the play was produced, entitled *The Painful Adventures of Pericles, Prynce of Tyre, being the true history of Pericles as it was lately presented by John Gower. Pericles* the play was published only in quarto form and was not included in a folio until the Third Folio of 1663.

## First half

The play opens with Pericles, prince of Tyre, seeking the hand of the daughter of King Antiochus of Antioch. To determine the best potential husband, the king has posed a riddle whose answer, Pericles deduces, reveals that the king has long been engaged in an incestuous relationship with his own daughter. Pericles promptly flees Antioch but is pursued by an assassin. Knowing what he knows, Pericles is in danger and decides to wander the world rather than return to Tyre. He finds himself in famine-struck Tarsus, where he brings food relief to the grateful governor Cleon and his wife Dionyza.

## Second half

Pericles's next stop is Pentapolis, where he is saved from a shipwreck by fishermen and takes part in a tournament for

Princess Thaisa, which he wins, and the two are wed. When they receive news that the incestuous King Antiochus and his daughter have been killed by a thunderbolt in punishment for their corruption, Pericles and his pregnant wife set sail for the now-safe Tyre. Their ship is struck by a storm and Thaisa dies giving birth to Pericles's daughter, Marina. Thaisa's body is buried at sea in a sealed chest with a note identifying her. When the chest washes up on the shores of Ephesus, the physician Cerimon brings Thaisa back to life. Revived from the dead, Pericles's wife dedicates herself to Diana, goddess of chastity.

Meanwhile, Pericles entrusts his daughter Marina to the care of Cleon and Dionyza in Tarsus and returns alone to Tyre.

We are told by Gower that fourteen years pass and Pericles's daughter Marina has blossomed into a beautiful young woman—much to the distaste of her foster mother. Fearing her own son is being eclipsed by Marina, Dionyza plots to have her killed. However, before the deed is done, Marina is kidnapped by pirates and sold to a brothel in Mytilene. Against the odds the young woman manages to preserve her virginity and so terrifies the brothel's customers that she is quickly off-loaded onto the governor Lysimachus.

Hearing of his daughter's supposed death, a disconsolate Pericles set off from Tyre once more to wander the seas. He finds himself in Mytilene where Marina is commanded to sing for him. Spotting her resemblance to his dead wife, Pericles questions her and it is soon revealed that she is his daughter.

In a dream Pericles is told to go to Ephesus by the goddess Diana. There he relates his experiences to a priestess who turns out to be Thaisa. The couple are blissfully reunited. Pericles installs his daughter and her new husband Lysimachus as king and queen of Tyre, while planning to rule Thaisa's kingdom of Pentapolis alongside his wife.

# *Timon of Athens (with Thomas Middleton)*

This incomplete play appeared in the First Folio of 1623 but there are questions as to how reliable its source is. Some scholars believe that a stylistic analysis points to a collaboration with fellow Jacobean playwright Thomas Middleton.

## First half

The play's eponymous character is a wealthy gentleman of Athens known for his generosity. He is surrounded by well-wishers, but soon Timon's cash reserves run low, and his creditors call in their debts. Penniless, Timon seeks help from his friends, only to be refused again and again. He hosts one last banquet, but instead of food and drink he serves hot water and stones, which he throws in the faces of his grasping guests.

## Second half

With his only true friend, Alcibiades, in exile, Timon goes to live in a cave as a hermit. One day, as he digs for roots, he unearths hidden treasure. Rather than keep it for himself, he gives it away—not to his former friends, the upstanding citizens of Athens, but to bandits, his loyal servant Flavius, and to Alcibiades to help raise an army against the senators of Athens. Alcibiades is victorious, but it is too late: Timon has died, taking his bitter hatred of humanity to the grave.

# The Winter's Tale

Though today's producers might be tempted to rename this play *When Bears Attack,* Shakespeare chose a no-less-playful title for his day, suggesting that the action and adventure in *The Winter's Tale* might all be part of a story told on a cold, blustery night.

## First half

Polixenes, king of Bohemia, has been visiting his much-loved childhood friend Leontes, King of Sicily, for nine months and is planning to return home. Leontes and his wife Hermione implore Polixenes to stay a while longer. Leontes is unsuccessful in his request, but Polixenes is more responsive to the queen's.

Leontes instantly becomes suspicious of Polixenes and Hermione's relationship and convinces himself that his pregnant wife carries the child of his friend. Leontes' transformation from adoring husband and friend to jealous monster is swift and brutal. He orders his servant Camillo to poison Polixenes and imprisons his wife. Camillo and the Bohemian king escape, but Queen Hermione is not so fortunate. First her young, sensitive son Mamillius dies with grief, then her husband rejects his new infant daughter. Unable to take any more tragedy, Hermione herself expires, and Leontes is left alone with the realization that he has greatly wronged his nearest and dearest.

## Second half

At the behest of Leontes, Antigonus, husband of the queen's closest friend Paulina, agrees to abandon the infant princess in some remote place. Antigonus chooses Bohemia, where, as he walks away from the abandoned girl, he falls prey to Shakespeare's best-known stage direction: "Exit, pursued by bear." The secret of the child's identity dies with him—or so it seems.

The baby is found and raised by a kindly shepherd who calls her Perdita. Though she has been brought up as a simple peasant, Perdita's unusual grace and dignity attracts the attention of Florizel, the prince of Bohemia. His father Polixenes is none too pleased when he hears of his son and the shepherdess, but his servant Camillo, touched by their love, takes them to Sicily and into the protection of the heartbroken and thoroughly repentant Leontes.

The king is struck by Perdita's resemblance to his wife and is quickly overwhelmed with grief. Seeing this, Paulina shows the king a statue of his wife that is uncannily lifelike. After a particularly silly scene in which everyone admires the "living" statue, it is revealed to be Hermione, whose death was faked to escape her husband's wrath. Seeing Leontes's grief and her long-lost daughter, Hermione forgives her husband, and the family is reunited. With perfect timing Polixenes shows up. Leontes apologizes, and all are friends again. Florizel and Perdita are wed.

# The Tempest

Perhaps the most accomplished of his romances, *The Tempest* is also the last play attributed exclusively to Shakespeare.

## First half

True to its name, this play begins with a fierce storm, which threatens to sink the ship of King Alonso of Naples. On an island nearby, the delighted magician Prospero explains to his daughter Miranda that his spirit servant Ariel is responsible for the storm.

He reveals the truth of who they are and how they came to be on the island. When Miranda was just a baby, Prospero had been the Duke of Milan but was usurped by his wicked brother Antonio with the aid of Alonso of Naples. Father and daughter were then exiled on a leaking boat. Fate smiled on them, and they washed up on the shores of their enchanted tropical island, where Ariel and the monstrous Caliban became their servants.

Under Prospero's instruction, Ariel continues to torment the island's shipwrecked new arrivals—setting them against each other, tempting them with food that disappears as soon as they try to eat it, and telling Alonso that his son Ferdinand has drowned because of his former sins. Ariel goes on to chastise Alonso and Antonio for exiling Prospero from Milan.

## Second half

Ferdinand has not drowned, however. Instead, he has washed up on a different part of the island and had the opportunity to meet and fall in love with Miranda, albeit while enslaved by Prospero.

Elsewhere, the disgruntled Caliban plots against his master, Prospero, with Antonio's servant Stephano and Alonso's jester Trinculo. Their plan is to remove Prospero from power and install Stephano as the island's ruler. They are lured to Prospero's cell and there try on lavish outfits that Ariel has provided. Prospero then unleashes spirits in the form of vicious dogs that chase the terrified would-be usurpers.

Ariel reports back to Prospero that his brother Antonio and his ally Alonso are showing signs of genuine remorse for how they have used him in the past. The old magician decides that he has had enough vengeance and sends for them. Then, having bound them all in a magic circle, one by one has his final say on their treachery and forgives them. Only when he has finished does he reveal his true identity. Alonso reinstates Prospero's title of Duke of Milan, and in turn, Prospero reveals that Ferdinand is still alive and intent on marrying Miranda.

In a final act of goodwill, Prospero pardons Caliban and grants him and Ariel their freedom.

# Cymbeline

Cymbeline ruled Britain from around 30 B.C. until the turn of the first millennium. This play, however, is less concerned with the historic details of the king's life than it is with the melodrama it creates for Cymbeline's daughter Imogen and for his scheming second wife and her stepson Cloten. The play's namesake ends up with a relatively minor role.

## First half

Cymbeline and his queen wish Imogen to marry Cloten, but instead she chooses to marry the unfortunately named Posthumus. As punishment for this disobedience, her new husband is banished to Italy.

In Rome, Posthumus boasts to his friend Iachimo about his distant wife's beauty and fidelity, prompting Iachimo to bet he could seduce her. The wager set, Iachimo sets sail on this elaborate mission but rather than actively trying to seduce Imogen, he tells her that her husband is unfaithful and later creeps around her bedroom while she sleeps, taking note of its details and stealing a bracelet. He brings these back to Posthumus by way of proof that his seduction was successful. The enraged husband then sends his servant Pisanio to kill Imogen. Upon seeing the beautiful young lady, Pisanio cannot carry out the order and instead warns her to disguise herself—you guessed it—as a boy, and to seek refuge in Wales.

## Second half

Then, poor Imogen's horrendous stepbrother Cloten decides to pursue her. He dresses as Posthumus, with the intention of forcing himself on her, but is intercepted by Imogen's long-lost brother, who was abducted years ago and raised under another name. Cloten is beheaded in the resulting skirmish.

Next, Imogen unwittingly takes a potion that makes her sleep deeply, giving the appearance of death (much like Juliet; see page 73). When she awakes to find Cloten's body beside her, she mistakes it for Posthumus. Then the real and very repentant Posthumus returns to England (disguised as a beggar after a short stint as a prisoner of the Romans) and is joyfully reunited with his wife.

Cymbeline, who has been rather conspicuously absent from most of the drama, gets to tie up the loose bits and deliver the play's happy ending, which also involves the wicked queen's inevitable death from "apoplexy"—whatever that is.

# The Two Noble Kinsmen (with John Fletcher)

There is a large question mark over the authenticity of this play, though it is widely agreed that Shakespeare at least cowrote it. The play is thought to have been written between 1613 and 1614 and was originally attributed to John Fletcher, coauthor of *Henry VIII* (see page 143). It did not appear in the First Folio of 1623 but did make it into a quarto in 1634 with an author credit naming both Fletcher and Shakespeare. There are two quite distinct styles in evidence in the play, one poetic (thought to be Shakespeare) and one plainer and more linear (Fletcher).

Based on the first of Geoffrey Chaucer's *Canterbury Tales*, "The Knight's Tale," the story is set in ancient Greece during the reign of Theseus but, like its source text, reads much more like a medieval chivalric romance.

## First half

Loyal cousins Palamon and Arcite are nephews of the villain-ous King Creon, enemy of King Theseus of Athens. Following a war between their kingdoms, the cousins are taken prisoner. While awaiting sentence in jail both have the opportunity to see Emilia, the beautiful daughter of Theseus—and both instantly fall in love with her. Thus a bitter rivalry begins between the two and all their former pledges of loyalty and love are fast forgotten.

Arcite is sentenced to banishment but soon returns to Athens and enters Emilia's service in disguise. Palamon gets a prison sentence but manages to escape with the help of the jailer's daughter, who falls in love with him to the point of madness. (She is later wooed out of her ravings by a charac-ter aptly called the "Wooer," and the two marry at the play's conclusion.)

## Second half

Arcite and Palamon face off in the forest, but their duel is interrupted by Theseus. Following the wishes of his wife and his daughter Emilia, he pardons them, but on condition that they fight a formal duel a month hence. The winner can marry Emilia, and the loser will face execution.

A month passes, and the two meet for their formal duel for Emilia's hand. Arcite wins but is crushed to death under his horse. With his dying breath he and Palamon reconcile, and Arcite gives Emilia to his friend to marry.

The play wasn't included in Shakespeare's canon until the latter half of the twentieth century and was first performed by the Royal Shakespeare Company in 1986.

# Henry VIII
# (with John Fletcher)

This was Shakespeare's last history play and was written after the death of Henry's daughter Queen Elizabeth I, so it marks not only the end of the Tudor era but the end of the Globe's glory days, too. It concentrates on the middle years of Henry's reign, up to the birth of Elizabeth. Shakespeare does not shy away from portraying the king as a despot but nor does he show the full extent of Henry's megalomania and the destruction it caused; while he covers the king's divorce from Katherine of Aragon, he does not mention England's subsequent devastating break with the church of Rome.

There is evidence that Shakespeare wrote this play in collaboration with John Fletcher, and a 1634 edition of the drama names them both as authors.

## First half

The play captures the pomp of Henry's court, while showing it to be a veneer hiding the darker political ambitions of certain nobles. The Duke of Buckingham and Lord Abergavenny are plotting to discredit the king's chief adviser, the Catholic Cardinal Wolsey. The king has separated from Katherine of Aragon on the grounds that she has not produced an heir and he targets Anne Bullen (Boleyn). Wolsey discovers a legal loophole that would allow the king to annul his marriage entirely. However, the king discovers that Wolsey is not acting entirely in his best interests. Wolsey has asked the Pope to delay the annulment and is trying to get Anne Bullen out of the picture—and is helping himself to state funds along the way. The king dismisses Wolsey and marries Anne in a lavish ceremony.

## Second half

Wolsey dies, and the king's enemies shift focus and accuse the recently appointed Archbishop of Canterbury, Thomas Cranmer, of heresy. Henry grants him immunity and asks him to be godfather to his newly born daughter Elizabeth. At her christening ceremony, the play's conclusion, Cranmer speaks about the new princess and the glories she will one day bring to England (though her father was still very much hoping for the arrival of a male heir).

The first Globe Theatre burned down in 1613 during a performance of *Henry VIII* when a spark from a cannonball set fire to the thatched roof. The theater was rebuilt the next year with a tile roof. The building was closed down by the Puritans in 1642 and demolished in 1644.

# "Knock, knock—who's there?"

# A Glossary
# of Major Characters

With thirty-eight plays, each crammed with characters, a complete list would be a book in its own right. For that reason I have listed only the most central characters of each play below in alphabetical order.

- **Aaron**—an evil Moor and the lover and partner in crime of Tamora, queen of the Goths, in *Titus Andronicus*. He incites most of the other evil characters to do violence against the Andronicus family.

- **Don Adriano de Armado**—a comic character in *Love's Labour's Lost*. His name is thought to be a jibing play on *armada*, as in the Spanish Armada.

- **Duke of Albany**—the relatively honorable husband of the Princess Goneril in *King Lear*.

🎭 **Alcibiades**—the only true friend of Timon of Athens, he is a soldier who rebels when one of his officers is wrongly sentenced to death.

🎭 **Alonso**—the King of Naples and ally to Prospero's usurping brother Antonio in *The Tempest*. His son Ferdinand marries Prospero's daughter Miranda.

🎭 **Angelo**—a saintly character who deputizes for the duke of Vienna in *Measure for Measure*. He is quickly corrupted by power and his desire for the chaste Isabella.

🎭 **Anne Bullen**—better known to history as Anne Boleyn, she is a lady-in-waiting to Katherine of Aragon and becomes King Henry's second wife in *Henry VIII*.

🎭 **Anne Page**—the daughter of Master and Mistress Page in *The Merry Wives of Windsor*. She is in love with Fenton, but her father wishes her to marry Slender, and her mother wishes her to marry Caius.

🎭 **Antigonus**—a servant of the jealous King Leontes in *The Winter's Tale*. He takes the infant princess, Perdita, to Bohemia and is killed by a bear.

🎭 **Antipholus of Ephesus**—the long-lost twin brother of Antipholus of Syracuse, with whom he is often confused in *The Comedy of Errors*.

**Antipholus of Syracuse**—in the reverse situation to the previous Antipholus.

**Antonio**—the title character, although not the central one, of *The Merchant of Venice*. He borrows money to give to his best friend Bassanio. When he cannot repay his debt, the Jewish moneylender Shylock demands a pound of Antonio's flesh.

**Antonio**—the usurping brother of the sorcerer Prospero in *The Tempest*.

**Arcite**—along with Palamon, title character of *The Two Noble Kinsmen*. Their friendship is tested in a quarrel for the love of Emilia.

**Ariel**—a spirit controlled, but eventually freed, by Prospero the magician in *The Tempest*.

**Queen Katherine of Aragon**—the first wife of King Henry in *Henry VIII*. She falls from grace, is divorced by the king, and dies. She is succeeded by Anne Bullen.

**Aufidius**—leader of the Volscians and archenemy of the titular hero in *Coriolanus*.

❧ **Banquo**—an army captain in *Macbeth* who hears the three witches' prophecies about Macbeth's rise to power and that of his own sons. He is later murdered but returns as a ghost to haunt Macbeth.

❧ **Bassanio**—the main male character in *The Merchant of Venice*. His friend Antonio financially supports his conquest of Portia.

❧ **Beatrice**—witty and sharp-tongued, she is a central character in *Much Ado About Nothing*. She falls in love with Benedick.

❧ **Benedick**—a central character in *Much Ado About Nothing*. He falls in love with Beatrice, and the two engage in some memorable verbal sparring.

❧ **Berowne**—a lord of Navarre in *Love's Labour's Lost*. He falls in love with Rosaline, thus breaking his oath to avoid women and live a studious life.

❧ **Bertram**—the Count of Roussillon in *All's Well That Ends Well*. He is married, against his will, to Helena on the order of the King of France. He abandons her and tries to annul their marriage.

❧ **Bianca**—the younger sister of Katherine in *The Taming of the Shrew*. She is loved by Gremio and Hortensio and eventually marries Lucentio.

- **Nick Bottom**—a weaver and amateur performer who rehearses with his acting troupe in the forest in *A Midsummer Night's Dream*. Puck transforms Bottom's head into that of an ass, and the enchanted fairy queen, Titania, falls in love with him.

- **Brutus**—also known as Marcus Brutus in *Julius Caesar*, he conspires against Caesar and ultimately stabs him.

- **Buckingham**—this character appears in both *Henry VI, Part 3* and *Richard III*. Initially, he is a co-conspirator with the evil Richard, but he is eventually rejected by him when he becomes king and is then murdered on Richard's orders.

- **Julius Caesar**—the title character of *Julius Caesar*, an emperor of Rome who is stabbed in the Capitol by conspirators, including Brutus, on the Ides of March.

- **Caius Cassius**—a central character in *Julius Caesar*. He recruits Brutus into a conspiracy against the emperor.

- **Calchas**—Cressida's father in *Troilus and Cressida*. He defects to the Greeks and negotiates his daughter's exchange for a Trojan prisoner.

# A Glossary of Major Characters

🏵 **Caliban**—the monstrously deformed son of the witch Sycorax and slave to the magician Prospero in *The Tempest*.

🏵 **Michael Cassio**—in *Othello*, Iago persuades Othello that Cassio is having an affair with his wife, Desdemona.

🏵 **Claudio**—falls in love with and is engaged to Hero but is persuaded, wrongly, that she has been unfaithful in *Much Ado About Nothing*.

🏵 **Claudio**—the brother of Isabella in *Measure for Measure*. He is sentenced to death for fornication under Angelo's reign in place of the Duke of Vienna.

🏵 **King Claudius**—the uncle and stepfather of the title character in *Hamlet*. He murders his brother Old Hamlet, assumes his throne, and marries his queen, Gertrude.

🏵 **Cleopatra**—queen of Egypt and the lover of Roman leader Antony in *Antony and Cleopatra*. Formerly the lover of Julius Caesar, she commits suicide using a poisonous asp (snake).

🏵 **Cloten**—son of the queen and stepson to the king in *Cymbeline*, he is in love with his stepsister Imogen, who does not return his feelings.

- **Cordelia**—the only honest and loving daughter of *King Lear*. She is wrongly rejected by her father and marries the King of France. At the end of the play she is hanged on Edmund's instructions.

- **Coriolanus**—the central character of *Coriolanus*. He earns this title in recognition of his skill at fighting the Volscians in Coriolai. A proud leader, he is rejected by the plebeians of Rome, and so joins his old enemies against the city.

- **The Duke of Cornwall**—the wicked, power-hungry husband of Regan in *King Lear*. He puts out the eyes of the king's loyal friend Gloucester.

- **Cressida**—daughter of a Trojan defector and one of the titular characters in *Troilus and Cressida*. The Trojan prince Troilus falls in love with her, but she does not return his feelings.

- **Cymbeline**—the title character of *Cymbeline,* he is king of the Britons and father to Imogen, Guiderus, and Arviragus. He has a relatively minor role in the story.

**Demetrius**—in love with Hermia at the start of *A Midsummer Night's Dream* and much beloved of Helena, whom he later marries.

**Desdemona**—the protagonist's wife in *Othello*. Her husband is tricked into believing she has been unfaithful and suffocates her.

**Dromio of Ephesus**—servant to Antipholus of Ephesus and long-lost twin brother of Dromio of Syracuse, with whom he is often confused, in *The Comedy of Errors*.

**Dromio of Syracuse**—as above but in reverse.

**Duncan**—the king of Scotland, murdered by the title character in Macbeth

**Edgar**—the worthy, legitimate son of Gloucester in *King Lear*. He is incriminated by his wicked half-brother and forced out of his father's house. He disguises himself as "Poor Tom" and stays close by.

**Edmund**—a calculating villain intent on taking power from his adoring father Gloucester and his half-brother Edgar in *King Lear*.

**Egeon**—a merchant from Syracuse and father of the separated twins Antipholus of Ephesus and Antipholus of Syracuse in *The Comedy of Errors*.

**Emilia**—the wife of wicked Iago and maidservant of Desdemona in *Othello*. At her husband's behest she steals Desdemona's handkerchief and unwittingly sets in motion a plot against Othello. She is murdered by her husband at the end of the play.

**Sir John Falstaff**—one of the most famous supporting roles in Shakespeare. He appears in *Henry IV, Part 1*; *Henry IV, Part 2*; and *The Merry Wives of Windsor*. In the Henry plays he is the carousing, corrupting friend of prince Hal and is eventually rejected by him. In *Merry Wives* he attempts to seduce two married women for financial gain. His death is reported in *Henry V*, although he is not a character in that play.

**Flavius**—the loyal steward to Timon in *Timon of Athens*, who tries desperately to prevent his master's collapse into poverty.

**Florizel**—the son of Polixines, king of Bohemia, in *The Winter's Tale*. He elopes with the shepherdess Perdita when his father prevents their marriage.

**Queen Gertrude**—the mother of Hamlet and the queen of Denmark in *Hamlet*. She marries Claudius, the brother and murderer of her first husband.

**Gloucester**—the father of Edgar and Edmund in *King Lear*. He has his eyes put out by the Duke of Cornwall for his loyalty to the old king.

**Goneril**—the cruel, power-mad eldest daughter in *King Lear*. She is married to the Duke of Albany.

**Hamlet**—the central character of *Hamlet,* he is the famously philosophical and procrastinating Prince of Denmark, called on to avenge his father's murder by his uncle Claudius. His is the biggest role of any in Shakespeare.

**Helena**—the ward of the Countess of Rousillon and the central character of *All's Well That Ends Well*. She married the countess's son Bertram against his will but eventually wins his love.

**Helena**—a young Athenian woman formerly loved by Demetrius, she has been rejected by him at the start of *A Midsummer Night's Dream*.

**Henry Bolingbroke**, later **King Henry IV**—he leads a revolt against King Richard in *Richard II* and is the title character of *Henry IV, Part 1,* and *Henry IV, Part 2,* which chart the rebellions against him and his difficult relationship with his eldest son, Hal, later Henry V.

**King Henry V** (sometimes called the Prince of Wales, Prince Henry, Hal, or just Harry)—a central character in *Henry IV, Part 1* and *Henry IV, Part 2* and the title character of *Henry V.* As a young prince he falls under the influence of the reprobate Falstaff, but when he ascends the throne, he rejects his former friend and leads the English to victory at Agincourt.

**King Henry VI**—the title character of *Henry VI, Parts 1, 2,* and *3,* is a weak and ineffectual king who is eventually overthrown and murdered.

**King Henry VII**—previously the **Earl of Richmond**, he led the rebellion against the cruel rule of *Richard III* and ultimately succeeds him as king.

**King Henry VIII**—the central character of the play *Henry VIII* and the father of Shakespeare's first royal patron, Queen Elizabeth I. He is portrayed as a wise and strong ruler rather than a despot.

**Hermia**—elopes with Lysander against the wishes of her father in *A Midsummer Night's Dream*. She is pursued into the forest by Demetrius, who in turn is pursued by Helena.

❦ **Hermione**—the wife of King Leontes in *The Winter's Tale*. Her husband believes she has been unfaithful and persecutes her. She fakes her own death to escape him and returns from the dead at the end of the play.

❦ **Hero**—falls in love with Claudio in *Much Ado About Nothing*. She is falsely accused of infidelity before their wedding and is abandoned at the altar by Claudio.

❦ **Horatio**—the loyal friend and confidant of the prince in *Hamlet*.

❦ **Hotspur** or **Harry Percy**—the brave but hot-headed foil to Hal and leader of the rebel forces in *Henry IV, Part 1*.

❦ **Iago**—the villain of *Othello*, he deceives the title character into believing that his wife, Desdemona, has been unfaithful to him. Othello then murders Desdemona in a jealous rage. Iago has the most lines of any character in the play.

❦ **Imogen**—the king's daughter in *Cymbeline*. Imogen's husband, Posthumus, is tricked into believing she has been unfaithful and orders his servant to kill her. Luckily for her, he then sees the error of his ways.

❧ **Isabel/Isabella**—a novice nun who pleads for the life of her brother Claudio in *Measure for Measure*. Claudio has been condemned to die by Angelo on a charge of fornication. The corrupt Angelo promises to free her brother if Isabel will give him her virginity.

❧ **Julia**—in love with Proteus, one of *The Two Gentlemen of Verona*. She pursues him to Milan disguised as a boy, only to discover he has shifted is affections to his best friend's girl, Silvia.

❧ **Juliet**—the daughter of Capulet, she falls in love with Romeo, the son of her father's enemy Montague, with tragic results in *Romeo and Juliet*.

❧ **Katherine** (also Kate)—the "shrew" from the title of *The Taming of the Shrew*, who is tamed by the domineering Petruchio.

❧ **Laertes**—the son of the king's chief adviser Polonius and the brother of Ophelia in *Hamlet*. He duels with and kills Hamlet in the final act.

# A Glossary of Major Characters

⚜ **Friar Laurence**—confidant to Romeo in *Romeo and Juliet*. His attempt to help the young couple backfires spectacularly and results in both their deaths.

⚜ **King Lear**—divides his kingdom between his two elder daughters, Regan and Goneril, who betray him, and mistakenly banishes his loyal youngest daughter, Cordelia, in *King Lear*. His ill-treatment drives him mad and ultimately to his death.

⚜ **Leontes**—the jealous king of Sicilia in *The Winter's Tale*. He wrongly suspects his wife, Hermione, of infidelity and compels her (seeming) death. He also banishes his newborn baby Perdita to the wilderness.

⚜ **Marcus Aemilius Lepidus**—one of the triumvirs, the three rulers of Rome after Caesar's death, in *Julius Caesar* and *Antony and Cleopatra*.

⚜ **Longaville**—along with Berowne and Dumaine, he is one of the three companions of the King of Navarre in *Love's Labour's Lost*.

⚜ **Lucentio**—falls in love with and marries Bianca, younger sister of Kate the "shrew" in *The Taming of the Shrew*. He disguises himself as a Latin master in order to woo her.

⚜ **Lysander**—in love with Hermia in *A Midsummer Night's Dream*.

**Lysimachus**—the governor of Mytilene, in *Pericles, Prince of Tyre*. He reunites the honorable Marina with her father, Pericles.

**Macbeth**—the central character in *Macbeth*. When he is told by three witches that he will reign over Scotland, he decides to hurry the prophesy along.

**Lady Macbeth**—the wife of Macbeth, she encourages her husband to murder the king of Scotland and take his crown but is driven mad as a consequence and dies, possibly through suicide.

**Macduff**—the thane of Fife and former friend of Macbeth, who murders Macduff's wife and children. He fights on Malcolm's side and kills Macbeth.

**Malcolm**—the eldest son of the murdered king of Scotland, Duncan, in *Macbeth*.

**Malvolio**—steward to, and secretly in love with, Olivia in *Twelfth Night*. He is imprisoned as a madman.

**Mark Antony**—turns the citizens of Rome against Julius Caesar's killers and becomes a triumvir in *Julius Caesar*. His romance with Cleopatra leads to a split with Rome in *Antony and Cleopatra*.

🐝 **Mercutio**—the witty friend of Romeo in *Romeo and Juliet*. He delivers the play's famous Queen Mab speech and is later killed by Juliet's cousin Tybalt.

🐝 **King of Navarre**—along with his three courtiers, Berowne, Dumaine, and Longaville, the king vows to study and fast for three years in *Love's Labour's Lost*.

🐝 **Oberon**—king of the fairies in *A Midsummer Night's Dream*. He plays tricks on a number of characters in the forest, including his wife Titania.

🐝 **Octavius Caesar**—one of the triumvirs, the three rulers of Rome after Julius Caesar's death, in *Julius Caesar*, and ultimately goes to war against Mark Antony in *Antony and Cleopatra*.

🐝 **Olivia**—a wealthy countess in *Twelfth Night*. She is loved by Orsino but falls in love with Cesario (the lady, Viola, in disguise).

🐝 **Ophelia**—the former lover of the title character in *Hamlet*. She rejects Hamlet on the orders of her father. She goes mad following her father's death at Hamlet's hands and drowns herself.

🐝 **Orlando**—the lover of Rosalind on the run in the forest in *As You Like It*.

🐝 **Orsino**—in love with Olivia and is loved in turn by Viola, who enters his service disguised as a boy, Cesario, in *Twelfth Night*.

🐝 **Othello**—the Moorish title character of *Othello*. He is a general in the Venetian army who is deceived by Iago that his wife, Desdemona, is having an affair. His jealousy drives him to murder.

🐝 **Palamon**—a title character, along with Arcite in *The Two Noble Kinsmen*. They both fall in love with Emilia and face each other in a duel for her affections at the play's conclusion.

🐝 **Don Pedro**—the prince of Aragon in *Much Ado About Nothing*. His brother Don John unsuccessfully attempts to implicate him in an infidelity scandal as revenge for being defeated by Don Pedro in battle.

🐝 **Perdita**—the daughter of King Leontes in *The Winter's Tale* who believes that his wife has been unfaithful, and his servant abandons the newborn Perdita in Bohemia. She grows up to marry Florizel and is reconciled to her father.

# A Glossary of Major Characters

🌸 **Pericles**—the central character of *Pericles*. Following a series of unfortunate events, Pericles loses his wife and his daughter, but is eventually reunited with them.

🌸 **Petruchio**—the smooth-talking central male character in *The Taming of the Shrew*, who "tames" the title character, Katherine.

🌸 **Polixines**—the king of Bohemia in *The Winter's Tale*. His friend Leontes wrongly accuses him of having an affair with his wife Hermione.

🌸 **Polonius**—the chief adviser in the court of King Claudius in *Hamlet*, and the father of Ophelia and Laertes. He is stabbed to death by Hamlet.

🌸 **Portia**—the romantic lead female character in *The Merchant of Venice*. Portia disguises herself as a lawyer, Balthasar, to prevent the moneylender Shylock from claiming his "pound of flesh" from Antonio.

🌸 **Posthumus Leonatus** (or just Posthumus)—defies the king, marrying the princess Imogen, and is banished to Italy in *Cymbeline*. He is tricked into believing that Imogen is unfaithful, and he orders his servant to travel to England to kill her.

❧ **Prospero**—the central character of *The Tempest*. Prospero is the former Duke of Milan who was usurped by his brother. He has become a sorcerer and lives on a magical island with his daughter, Miranda, and two servants—the spirit Ariel and monstrous Caliban.

❧ **Proteus**—one of *The Two Gentlemen of Verona*. At the start of the play he is in love with Julia, but later falls for his best friend's sweetheart, Silvia, sabotages their relationship, and attempts to claim her as his own by force.

❧ **Puck**—a famously mischievous fairy and the servant of Oberon in *A Midsummer Night's Dream*. Puck casts spells over the young lovers in the forest.

❧ **Regan**—the callous second daughter in *King Lear*. She is married to the equally callous duke of Cornwall.

❧ **King Richard II**—the title character of *Richard II*, he is a weak king who is deposed and ultimately murdered.

❧ **Richard, Duke of Gloucester**, later **Richard III**—the third son of Richard, Duke of York, Richard is first a minor character in *Henry VI, Part 2*. He becomes more prominent and is shown to be a brave soldier in *Henry VI, Part 3*. In *Richard III* he is characterized as a cold-hearted, power-mad villain and is Shakespeare's most famously evil creation.

**Romeo**—a title character in *Romeo and Juliet* and the son of Montague, he falls in love with Juliet, the daughter of his father's enemy Capulet, with tragic results.

**Rosalind**—the biggest female character in Shakespeare. She is banished to the Forest of Arden where she disguises herself as a boy, Ganymede, in *As You Like It*.

**Sebastian**—the twin brother of Viola, the two are shipwrecked and separated in *Twelfth Night*. He is frequently mistaken for Viola's male persona, Cesario. The wealthy Olivia marries him under such a misapprehension.

**Shylock**—a Jewish moneylender who claims a pound of Antonio's flesh when he cannot repay a loan in *The Merchant of Venice*.

**Silvia**—the faithful lover of Valentine in *The Two Gentlemen of Verona*, she is aggressively pursued by his best friend, Proteus.

🦋 **Tamora**—the evil queen of the Goths in *Titus Andronicus,* who is locked in a vicious circle of revenge with the titular warrior.

🦋 **Timon**—the lead character in *Timon of Athens*. Timon's extravagant generosity earns him many false friends. When he falls on hard times, he finds no assistance forthcoming and becomes an embittered hermit.

🦋 **Titania**—the wife of Oberon and queen of the fairies in *A Midsummer Night's Dream*. She falls in love with Nick Bottom while both are under spells.

🦋 **Titus Andronicus**—the lead character in the bloody revenge tragedy *Titus Andronicus*, he is driven mad by his enemy Tamora, queen of the Goths, and eventually takes his revenge by killing her sons, cooking them, and fooling her into eating them.

🦋 **Troilus**—a young Trojan prince who falls in love with Cressida during the Trojan War in *Troilus and Cressida*. She falls in love with another, leading him to rage through the enemy camp, sparking a fierce battle.

🦋 **Tybalt**—the cousin of Juliet in *Romeo and Juliet*. His fiery temper leads him to kill Mercutio, and he in turn is killed by Romeo.

# A Glossary of Major Characters

✦ **Valentine**—one of *The Two Gentlemen of Verona*. He falls in love with Silvia, the daughter of the duke of Milan, and is exiled in the forest where he becomes the leader of a band of robbers. His best friend Proteus attempts to steal Silvia away.

✦ **Vincentio**—the absentee Duke of Vienna in *Measure for Measure*. He appoints the corrupt Angelo to enforce some unpleasant laws and watches his replacement's conduct from afar, disguised as a friar. He returns to the action of the play when it appears that Angelo is seriously abusing his new powers.

✦ **Viola**—the shipwrecked twin of Sebastian in *Twelfth Night*. She disguises herself as a boy named Cesario and enters the service of her beloved Orsino. However, she is loved by another woman, Olivia, who falls for her persona as Cesario.

✦ **Three Witches**—also known as the "weird sisters," these three predict Macbeth's rise to the throne of Scotland and thus inspire him to hurry the process along by murdering King Duncan in *Macbeth*.

✦ **Cardinal Wolsey**—engineers the fall from grace of Buckingham and Katherine of Aragon, but falls from grace himself and dies in *Henry VIII*.

# Index of Famous Lines

A horse! A horse! My kingdom for a horse!
*RICHARD III* 5.4.7 AND 13 (RICHARD AT BATTLE OF BOSWORTH)

A little more than kin, and less than kind.
*HAMLET* 1.2.65 (HAMLET ON HIS RELATIONSHIP TO HIS UNCLE)

A plague o' both your houses.
*ROMEO AND JULIET* 3.1.92 (MERCUTIO AS HE DIES)

Alas, poor Yorick. I knew him, Horatio, a fellow of infinite jest, of most excellent fancy.
*HAMLET* 5.1.182–3 (HAMLET UPON DISCOVERING YORICK'S SKULL)

All is not well.
I doubt some foul play.
*HAMLET* 1.2.255–6 (HAMLET)

As Caesar loved me, I weep for him; as he was fortunate, I rejoice at it; as he was valiant, I honour him; but, as he was ambitious, I slew him.
*JULIUS CAESAR* 3.2.24–7 (BRUTUS)

As flies to wanton boys are we to the gods,
They kill us for their sport.
*KING LEAR* 4.1.38–9 (GLOUCESTER TO AN OLD MAN)

# Index of Famous Lines

Better a witty fool than a foolish wit.
*TWELFTH NIGHT* 1.5.90–2 (OLIVIA TO FESTE)

By the pricking of my thumbs,
Something wicked this way comes.
*MACBETH* 4.1.44–5 (SECOND WITCH)

Come not between the dragon and his wrath.
*KING LEAR* 1.1.123 (LEAR TO KENT)

Confusion now hath made his masterpiece.
*MACBETH* 2.3.66 (MACDUFF ON DUNCAN'S MURDER)

Conscience does make cowards of us all.
*HAMLET* 3.1.83 (HAMLET)

For a kingdom any oath may be broken.
*HENRY VI* 1.2.16 (EDWARD TO RICHARD OF YORK)

Frailty, thy name is woman.
*HAMLET* 1.2.146 (HAMLET)

Get thee to a nunnery. Why wouldst thou be a breeder of sinners?
*HAMLET* 3.1.121–2 (HAMLET TO OPHELIA)

Have more than thou showest,
Speak less than thou knowest,
Lend less than thou owest.
*KING LEAR* 1.4.116–18 (FOOL TO LEAR)

He can speak French; and therefore he is a traitor.
*HENRY VI, PART II* 4.2.161–2 (JACK CADE ON LORD STAFFORD)

How my achievements mock me!
*TROILUS AND CRESSIDA* 4.2.71 (TROILUS)

# "Knock, knock—who's there?"

I am a man
More sinned against than sinning.
*KING LEAR* 3.2.59–60 (LEAR TO KENT)

I am myself alone.
*HENRY VI* 5.6.83 (RICHARD OF GLOUCESTER)

I must be cruel only to be kind.
*HAMLET* 3.4.180 (HAMLET TO GERTRUDE)

I shall be loved when I am lacked.
*CORIOLANUS* 4.1.15 (CORIOLANUS TO HIS WIFE AND MOTHER)

I understand a fury in your words
But not the words.
*OTHELLO* 4.2.32–3 (DESDEMONA TO OTHELLO)

If it were done, when 'tis done, then 'twere well
It were done quickly.
*MACBETH* 1.7.1–2 (MACBETH)

Let me embrace thee, sour Adversity,
For wise me say it is the wisest course.
*HENRY VI* 3.1.24–5 (HENRY)

Misery acquaints a man with strange bedfellows.
*TEMPEST* 2.2.38-9 (TRINCULO)

Mislike me not for my complexion.
*MERCHANT OF VENICE* 2.1.1 (PRINCE OF MOROCCO TO PORTIA)

Now cracks a noble heart. Good night, sweet prince,
And flights of angels sing thee to thy rest.
*HAMLET* 5.2.368–9 (HORATIO ON HAMLET'S DEATH)

O beauty,
Till now I never knew thee.
HENRY VIII 1.4.75–6 (HENRY'S FIRST SIGHTING OF ANNE BULLEN)

Out, damned spot! Out, I say!
MACBETH 5.1.36 (LADY MACBETH)

Parting is such sweet sorrow
That I shall say good night till it be morrow.
ROMEO AND JULIET 2.2.14–5 (JULIET TO ROMEO)

Seems, madam? Nay, it is. I know not "seems."
HAMLET 1.2.76 (HAMLET TO GERTRUDE)

Shall I be plain? I want the bastards dead.
RICHARD III 4.2.18 (RICHARD ON HIS NEPHEWS)

Smooth runs the water where the brook is deep.
HENRY VI, PART II 3.1.53 (SUFFOLK TO LORDS)

Tempt not a desperate man.
ROMEO AND JULIET 5.3.59 (ROMEO TO PARIS)

The better part of valor is discretion, in which better art I have
saved my life.
HENRY IV, PART I, 5.4.118–20 (FALSTAFF)

The Devil can cite Scripture for his purpose.
MERCHANT OF VENICE 1.3.96 (ANTONIO TO BASSANIO)

The devil hath power
T'assume a pleasing shape.
HAMLET 2.2.601–2 (HAMLET)

The engineer
Hoist by his own petard.
    *HAMLET* 3.4.208–9 (HAMLET TO GERTRUDE)

The evil that me do lives after them,
The good is oft interred with their bones.
    *JULIUS CAESAR* 3.2.76–7 (MARK ANTONY TO THE PLEBEIANS)

The rest is silence.
    *HAMLET* 5.2.367 (HAMLET TO HORATIO)

The time is out of joint. O cursed spite,
That ever I was born to set it right.
    *HAMLET* 1.5.196–7 (HAMLET UPON MEETING HIS FATHER'S GHOST)

There's a divinity that shapes our ends,
Rough-hew them how we will.
    *HAMLET* 5.2.10–11 (HAMLET TO HORATIO)

There is no virtue like necessity.
    *RICHARD II* 1.3.278 (JOHN OF GAUNT TO BOLINGBROKE)

This above all: to thine own self be true,
And it must follow as the night the day
Thou canst not then be false to any man.
    *HAMLET* 1.3.78–80 (POLONIUS TO LAERTES)

This fellow is wise enough to play the fool.
    *TWELFTH NIGHT* 3.1.60 (VIOLA TO FESTE)

This is an art
Which does mend nature—change it rather—but
The art itself is nature.
    *WINTER'S TALE* 4.4.95–7 (POLIXENES TO PERDITA ON CROSS-BREEDING CROPS)

# Index of Famous Lines

This was the unkindest cut of all.
*JULIUS CAESAR* 3.2.184 (MARK ANTONY ON CAESAR'S MURDER)

Thus the native hue of resolution
Is sicklied o'er with the pale cast of thought.
*HAMLET* 3.1.84–8 (HAMLET)

Time goes on crutches till love hath all his rites.
*MUCH ADO ABOUT NOTHING* 2.1.336–7 (CLAUDIO TO DON PEDRO)

To do a great right, do a little wrong.
*MERCHANT OF VENICE* 4.1.214 (BASSANIO TO PORTIA)

We are such stuff
As dreams are made on.
*TEMPEST* 4.1.156–7 (PROSPERO TO MIRANDA)

We have seen better days.
*AS YOU LIKE IT* 2.7.120 (DUKE SENIOR TO ORLANDO)

When we are born we cry that we are come
To this great stage of fools.
*KING LEAR* 4.6.178–9 (LEAR TO GLOUCESTER)

Your face, my Thane, is as a book, where men
May read strange matters.
*MACBETH* 1.5.61–2 (LADY MACBETH TO HER HUSBAND)

# ENJOY THESE OTHER
# READER'S DIGEST BESTSELLERS

### I Used to Know That

Make learning fun again with these lighthearted pages that are packed with important theories, phrases, and those long-forgotten "rules" you once learned in school.

**Caroline Taggart**
**ISBN 978-0-7621-0995-1**

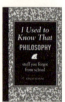

### I Used to Know That: Philosophy

Spanning over 2,000 years of philosophical thought, this book covers the main highlights, from Pythagoras to Socrates to Sartre. You'll get an overview of all the major theories, presented in an engaging format.

**Lesley Levene**
**ISBN 978-1-60652-323-0**

### I Used to Know That: Civil War

Taking you beyond the history book, this book brings to life colorful personal stories of heroes, brilliant military strategists, blunderers, guerillas, outright villains, spies, secret sympathizers on both sides, and their wives on the home front.

**Fred DuBose**
**ISBN 978-1-60652-244-8**

### I Used to Know That: Geography

It's hard to know everything about the interaction of diverse physical, biological, and cultural features of the Earth's surface. Explore all of it with this entertaining, easy-to-understand little book.

**Will Williams**
**ISBN 978-1-60652-245-5**

### i before e (except after c)

Featuring all the memory-jogging tips you'll ever need to know, this fun little book will help you recall hundreds of important facts using simple, easy-to-remember mnemonics from your school days.

**Judy Parkinson**
**ISBN 978-0-7621-0917-3**